Life As A Roller Coaster

The Mayhem of Bipolar

By Liz Rotherham

To Deb

keep shining your light!

Enjoy

Love Liz

x

Life As A Roller Coaster
ISBN: 978-1-5272-4744-4

First published in Great Britain
in 2019 through Amazon self-publishing
service Kindle Direct Publishing

Disclaimer: real names/places
have been changed to protect the identities.

Produced by samanthahoughton.co.uk

Dedication

For all those people coping with mental health issues and struggling to share their feelings and emotions.
For those feeling isolated, you are not alone and I hope this book helps you realise this.
For Darell who is my absolute rock.
Thank you and I love you zillions.

Author Bio

My name is Liz and I am Bipolar.

This book is a frank insight into my world.

I currently reside in an old country cottage with my partner, Darell and our two lovely springers, Charlie and Boris. We spend a great deal of time in the fresh air walking the dogs and enjoying the sheer beauty of the countryside. I also enjoy practicing mindfulness and meditation.

Throughout this book, my sister, Mum, nieces, ex-boss and partner have also given their perspective and thoughts about dealing with my Bipolar and explain just how challenging this can be.

I would like to help people understand how mental health problems can affect anyone and that no-one is alone and it is OK to share your emotions. One in four will experience some kind of mental health issue during their lives. It would appear that this statistic has increased over recent years since more people are speaking out and sharing their feelings.

I am extremely grateful to SANE mental health charity that has supported my book with their logo on the front page and a quote below from them. I am currently a media volunteer for SANE and plan to donate a percentage towards the charity to help them towards raising awareness with regards to the great work they do for mental health.

SANE is a leading UK mental health charity set up in 1986 to improve the quality of life for anyone affected by mental illness. Its three main aims are to raise awareness and combat stigma about mental illness, educating and campaigning to improve mental health services; to promote and host research into the causes and more effective treatments for mental illness at its flagship Prince of Wales International Centre for SANE Research; and to provide guidance and emotional support for people with mental health problems, their families and carers through its helpline, SANEline, Textcare and other services. For more information, please visit **www.sane.org.uk**.

By creating this book I hope to help people to understand the condition. I do not want in any way to make light of mental health issues as they are, indeed, very serious. However humour has always been a big part of my life and hence my story is told with an element of humour, please enjoy.

Acknowledgements

I started this book about 8 years ago and would not have been able to finish it without my amazing mentor Samantha Houghton. She has encouraged, supported and guided me over the last 6 months to make my dream happen, so I thank you from the bottom of my heart. To my partner, Darell, who has supported me over the last 10 years; Darell has been an absolute diamond and I don't know what I would have done without him. He has stood by me through thick and thin and has had to deal with some terrifying and upsetting circumstances. He is a strong, caring and beautiful person inside and out, he is my total rock and I love you Darell with all my heart.

To my Mum, who has had the worry of me for the last 48 years, she deserves a gold medal. Mum is an incredible woman and I thank you tremendously for your constant support and advice throughout my life.

To my step dad Trev, who arrived on the scene when I was 18, you have been like a real father to me and were a great support at my time of need back in 2003, and I am extremely grateful to you.

To my gorgeous sister, Kate, who makes me laugh constantly. Thank you for your support and always listening to me rant on, you are my best friend and I love you unconditionally. I know you have found it extremely difficult over the years, but admire how you have now overcome your fears in order to offer me continued support.

To my amazing two nieces, you are so special to me, don't ever change who you are. You are both so funny in different ways and I love your energy. Be the people you want to be and don't let anyone change your minds. I love you both zillions.

To my brother in law, Mark, who is just hilarious when he is on form. Thank you for your continued support over the years and being there for me at crucial times in my life.

To Robbie Cowling, if it weren't for you I wouldn't be here today. You spotted the signs back in 2003 and acted quickly to prevent something fatal happening. I am eternally grateful to you for that.

To all my grandparents who I love very much, I know you are with me and looking down on all of us. Thank you for all your support.

To my great friend Caroline who said to me once *'Liz if you put your mind to it, you can and will achieve anything in this world.'* I will never forget that comment and totally believe it. Thank you for being your creative self and a great friend.

Thank you to all of the NHS Staff who looked after me in hospital all the different times I was admitted, especially Ernie who looked after me back in 2003 like I was his own daughter and Cloud who has made my recent time in hospital more bearable. Thank you, you are both brilliant at your job. Also to my psychiatrist Dr Hamid who was extremely patient and supported me over all those years.

A huge thank you to all my friends, there are too many to list all of you! You have all been so supportive over the years, I love you all very much.

To Glynis, I thank you for your patience and support with my Bipolar; For also visiting me whilst in hospital and coming to my appointments with my psychiatrist. Thank you for believing in me that I can do a good job along with your continuous encouragement and hilarious sense of humour.

To Rhonda Byrne the author of *'The Secret'* after reading your book I understood about the laws of attraction and the universe. It is so true; what you give out in positivity comes back to you tenfold. This book changed my life. Thank you.

To Roy and my current work colleagues, you are all great and extremely supportive; Especially Roy for just being you and believing in me and not passing any judgement. I love my job which is helped by your open and honest nature and allowing me to just be me.

To Lorna Byrne who is an utter inspiration and helped me believe that angels are really true and are constantly trying to communicate and help us.

To my extended family, even if I have not personally spoken to you about my challenges I know you are there for me always via Mum or Kate and have supported me in all of your individual ways. Thank you.

To Will Polston, the founder of *'Make it Happen'* for making me believe that anything is possible and listening to me talk about my experience of Bipolar with no interruption or judgement and introducing me to people that have helped me on my journey. Thank you. To all the light-workers and holistic therapists out there, please continue doing your amazing and life changing work. Times are changing and more positivity is on its way.

Prologue

What a year 2002 was so far. I was being bullied at work, struggling in a controlling relationship, binge drinking like it was going out of fashion, dabbling in drugs and feeling totally crap about myself. I had just come back from what was supposed to be a dream holiday to the Maldives and all I wanted to do was cry and not leave my bed. This was not me, I was a positive person not this miserable wreck. What had happened? It felt like the whole world had caved in and all I wanted to do was hide away from everyone. The holiday was a disaster and my dream broken. I came back feeling totally useless with no enthusiasm to do anything. I didn't want to be around anyone so my sister took me to the doctor's, as I couldn't even muster up the strength to go by myself.

I bawled my eyes out at the doctors and my sister Kate had to speak for me. I kept wondering what on earth had happened to make me to be this uncontrollable sobbing person? It felt awful, as if the walls of hoover dam had finally broken and the river just flooded. I didn't even have time to worry about whether I was embarrassed or not - the doctor prescribed me Prozac! Why is it that doctors always think the best solution is medication? Did they not think counselling would be better? These questions started whizzing around in my brain, but I was too exhausted to even question what was happening and feebly took the medication. I had heard mixed comments about Prozac, however I did as the doctor requested and had two weeks off from work to try and sort myself out.

By Christmas I was kind of back to normal, whatever is classed to be normal these days. I went to see a Medium/psychic to try and help me, she said that there would be a massive change in my life around May time, huge in fact; and boy I was not expecting my life to turn head over heels quite as much as what happened next...

Contents

1

Take a Step Back

If I look back and try and recall when all the negative emotions started, I remember seeing my dad cowering behind the kitchen door whilst a man outside was shouting *'Come out and face me you coward - what are you, a man or a mouse?'* That was my best friends' dad and my Dad didn't move; he just stood there hiding behind the door whilst the guy continued to shout! I felt like screaming at my Dad saying *'grow some balls and go and face the man'* but I just watched with my mouth open, staring at both men. I later found out that Dad had been having an affair with his wife and yes it was my best friend at school's mum! My perfect world had been shattered and my Mum found out when the lady in question (who was supposedly her best friend too) came round and told her she was pregnant; how awful and shocking for my mum to deal with. My poor mum, I could only imagine what she was feeling, but she never said anything to me and kept a smile on her face at all times. She never showed any emotion and even forgave my Dad for what he did. I hated having to go back to school knowing that my best friend's mum had been sleeping with my dad. What did it all mean? I think even at that age I knew it was wrong and it had broken my mum's heart. I didn't want people talking behind my back at school and I am sure it was the hot topic on everyone's lips, as I used to get stared at and then people would cup their hands and smirk at me. I felt humiliated and so upset and kept thinking - was I to blame? Confusion set in and as that six year old at the time, I pushed it all to the back of my mind and pretended all was rosy.

It was bad enough that two girls were bullying me in my year that made me feel like crap, and they continued to call me names constantly, along with belittling me all the time. They used to be so nasty to me and leave me out of all the games. I used to spend my time with the younger kids and playing with them because they were so much kinder to me. I did however, feel very proud to be at the private school as my Granny Toby (Mum's Mum) was the Maths teacher, and my Auntie was one of the sports teachers there. They were both highly respected by the other teachers, so it felt like all the teachers took me under their wing and I was extremely well looked after. Gran told me that they had a new teacher there and apparently she came into the staffroom one lunchtime. The new teacher said that *'there is only one child at this school that won't settle down or calm down, and that is Liz Rotherham. She is a complete nightmare and irrepressible.'* Gran laughed and said to the troubled teacher that the girl she was ranting about was her beloved granddaughter, who she found very entertaining and likeable! That soon shut the teacher up; I was even causing trouble in my early years, all part of the fun hey! My favourite teachers were the headmaster and also the sports teacher. I think I had a secret crush on him, even at the age of 6 years old - what was I like! I remember the headmaster saying to me once *'you are full of spirit Liz don't ever let anyone change you'.* I loved that comment, and did feel very special even if other areas weren't so great.

I used to hang around with the boys a lot of the time due to the fact the two girls were bitchy to me and there were two boys in particular that I really liked but I couldn't make up my mind which one I liked the best. One of the boys was tall blonde and stocky and the other was short mousy haired and athletic. I used to always want to play kiss chase and run after the boys of which they always ran a mile. I'll never forget the time when I had the tall blonde one and his friends over to Mum's and they were more interested in watching football with my Mum than us girls, so my friends and I made notes and put them on string and gently lowered them from my bedroom window to outside the lounge window so that they could read them and come upstairs. Gosh anything to get attention – but they totally ignored us and we were not happy bunnies! I did love school and loved playing the musical instruments. The school used to put on an end of year play or musical and one year we did the Sound of Music. I was picked as Captain Von Trap and Mum got my hair cut the day before so short it looked like I had done it on purpose to play the part as a man! Everyone laughed but for once I didn't care as I loved singing and enjoyed myself thoroughly. I sang Edelweiss all by myself, and it went down a treat. I felt so proud as everyone clapped at the end. Mum always said I had a good voice and I used to love the choir.

My other Gran (Dad's Mum) lived in North Wales and we used to go and see Granny Peg a lot in my younger days. Granny Peg loved singing too and we always sang in the evening times whilst playing the piano. I loved visiting Granny Peg as she was such a kind, caring and funny person. She used to love baking and we used to help her make pies, cakes and buns. I spent hours in her garden with my sister Kate, running along the little paths that made up her garden. She had an allotment in her back garden which was huge and we used to pick all the vegetables for our dinner.

There were happy times in my childhood but I don't remember seeing Dad much, the ones that surface to my mind were the negative parts. We were on holiday in Greece and I went out on a surf board with Dad and one of our family friends, there wasn't enough room on the board so Dad sent me back to the shore and wouldn't take no for an answer. I pleaded with him to stay and cried and said there were jelly fish in the sea and they scared me and I didn't want to get stung, he ignored me and carried on swimming out to sea so I had to swim back on my own. By the time I got back I was stung from head to foot by jellyfish. The pain was unbearable and felt like someone was sticking needles into my body. It took ages for the stinging to calm down and Mum rubbed soothing cream to help, she was there (as always) to comfort me. I hate jellyfish even now, and if I see them on the beach I cut them into four! Charming hey - poor things do they deserve that sort of death?

The other time we were at the park, Mum, Dad and I and Dad was pushing me front ways on the swing, I was screaming and telling him to stop as I was scared but he laughed and pushed me higher. The next thing I knew, crack, I had landed on my chin on the pavement. I had to have stitches under my chin and have still got the scar today. Dad did have a nasty streak in him that occasionally surfaced and I wondered whether he enjoyed actually seeing me cry!

I was a very determined child and I remember once going on holiday to Spain again and the waves in the sea were extremely high and Mum advised me not to go in , I completely ignored her and went in anyhow as they looked fun. One wave completely knocked me off my feet and I lost all control, I hit my tooth on a rock and surfaced with my bikini top half off and feeling very dizzy. Some boys on the beach were laughing at me and I started crying as my tooth really hurt. Mum was not happy and told me to go and lie on the towel and when I hadn't stopped crying for about 10 mins she knew something was up and my tooth had been broken - whoops! I had to have it filed down at the dentist, that will teach me - always listen to your Mum!

The trip to the dentist was not much fun either, the injection really hurt and I pushed the dentist away and he shouted at me and scared the living daylights out of me, I know he might have been doing it for my own good but it put me off going to the dentist for 15 years and I am still very wary now. It's amazing how what happens when you are young has a fundamental effect on you in later life.

For Christmas one year Mum bought us a little kitten, we came down the stairs not sure what to expect and saw this little orange ball of fluff and we named him Orlando the Marmalade cat and Mum had also bought us a book called the same. I thought someone had actually written the book especially for our cat! So gullible I was!

We used to go down the stairs, Kate, me, and Orlando in a sleeping bag. Poor cat, we probably scared the hell out of him. We had so much fun until me being me, came down one day too fast and went crashing through the front door which was made of glass. Amazingly I didn't get told off and luckily didn't hurt myself. How I do not know, as we had completely destroyed the door; I hasten to add, we didn't do that again, nor were we allowed to have our sleeping bag slides down the stairs. Orlando was ruled by Hitler, (Hitler being Mum!) He used to go and put his foot into the lounge and Mum just used to give him a glaring look and you could see him cringe and withdraw his foot very carefully and run away!

Kate and I used to spend a lot of time round Granny Toby's and Grandad's after school whilst Mum was working. Every Sunday we had roast dinner round there and Grandad seemed like he took ages to cook the dinner. The kitchen also used to smell of dog mince as he boiled this for their dog Toby; hence the reason Gran was called Granny Toby. He was a gorgeous Labrador and we loved him so much. I used to play with him for ages and always pretend he was a horse and try and ride his back. Poor dog he was so patient with my sister and I.

Granny's garden was huge, and Kate and I used to play hide and seek for hours - I loved it and I felt happy and free. It was at Granny and Grandad's I was introduced to alcohol for the first time, Grandad was a nightmare but Kate and I loved it. We used to get a special treat, a glass of babycham (for people who remember that!) And I looked forward to it every week! Mum's sister and brother were very supportive too and I used to go to Bridget's, and Kate used to go to Stephen's, whilst Mum was trying to earn some extra money to support us.

In Bicknacre where I used to live, Kate and I played over the fields nearly every day after school, I tormented the life out of Kate and used to get great pleasure in chasing her with cow poo on a stick. Don't ask me why but I loved winding her up. Kate's nick-name was four eyes or double glazing as she wore glasses. I was so horrible to her and she used to end up crying and running to Mum a lot of the time. Why is it that sisters fight and argue and are so nasty to each other and then later in life become the best of friends? We also used to have hours of fun with our neighbours. Sometimes we were fighting with brooms and sticks against each other and then other times we were best mates.

That reminds me, how embarrassing is this? I was playing with our friends who were boys, I went indoors as nature was calling, sat on the toilet and left the door open for some bizarre reason. I was straining for a poo and guess what - the next thing I know is that there in front of me were 3 black faces pissing themselves laughing! I was mortified and wanted the ground to swallow me up. I could have died there and then.

Then one day it happened all over again with my dad, but worse. Standing in Granny Toby's house aged 9. Both Mum and Gran crying and I was pestering them as to why, then they told me the ground breaking news. *'Your Dad is leaving to go and have another life with a woman called Lucy!'* It was like I had been hit with a thunderbolt and I thought *'who the fuck is Lucy?'* Straight away I HATED her. Bitch, she has stolen my dad away from me - how dare she! I think now looking back, this was my first major breakdown as the news suddenly hit me and all that had happened a few years earlier with the stand -off, however for some reason I didn't cry. I pushed it to the back of my mind again as far away as possible and told everyone at school that my Dad had gone away on holiday and that he would be back soon; how wrong was I. Mum never discussed it, perhaps she thought what could she say to a nine year old as in those days there was no such thing as counselling for young people. I put all my emotions to the back of my mind and blocked it out like it had never happened, but realistically I was crying inside, just never showed it on the outside. I put up a mask so no-one could see what I truly felt.

When Dad left we had to move into a smaller house, how embarrassing was that? We swapped houses with someone over the road, so we could still see our house when we moved, great reminder. Although saying that, I wanted to be reminded as we had some fond memories playing with some local lads on the front lawn. I popped Kate's first space hopper on the rose bush, she hated me for that; she had only just bought it and was over the moon with it! Not for long hey! Anyway, going back to Dad, he moved with Lucy and her kids down to Swindon, so we used to go down there for the weekend. I hated it, all Lucy was interested in was her kids and what could be bought for them, and we were ignored. We weren't allowed in their rooms or to touch their toys. Dad was oblivious to how Kate and I felt as all he was interested in was pleasing Lucy. I went to visit under duress all the time and smiled sweetly when required as if nothing was wrong. I suppose looking back I kept all this inside and never spoke about it and Mum was never the wiser. Dad and Lucy had destroyed two marriages and I felt so sorry for her ex-husband.

Dad never paid any maintenance for us so we grew up with hardly any money. Mum had to borrow money off her parents to survive and get food for us. We couldn't afford heating, so Kate and I huddled around the gas fire getting ready for school. I wasn't unhappy, but I just got on with it as I was still pleased we had a house. I was just upset for mum, as she seemed to have lost her glow.

A couple of years later, I was about 11, I was walking along the road with Mum near the old Barclays in Chelmsford and saw a gentleman sitting in the corner desk. I randomly said to my mum *'why can't he be my Daddy'* and Mum laughed and said *'that's Trevor and he is happily married with three kids.'* I smiled, and the ironic thing was, 9 years later on he actually became my step dad, which is extremely spooky to think of a child saying this.

At school I failed my eleven plus, I was gutted as I so wanted to go to the high school, although the teachers said that I only missed it by 2%. Well great, that made me feel very special - basically that meant to me *'you are good but just not good enough!'* I felt very disappointed, where was I to go? I did not, for some reason, want to go to the local school as all the local kids were going there and in recent years they had all ganged up on me as I wanted to be a bit different and not follow the crowd.

I ended up going to Anglo European, which is a foreign language school. Goodness knows how I got into there, Mum says she has ties but hey, where the hell did they come from? I secretly think she slept with the head master! Mum that is a joke if you are reading this!

2

Schools Out

I was on the bus going to my new senior school and absolutely shitting my pants, how I didn't I don't know. I didn't talk to anyone, and there was so much noise. It seemed like everyone knew everyone and I was the only one who didn't. I fought back the tears and remained brave but my palms were sweaty and I felt sick. My stomach was doing somersaults and I thought any minute I was going to pass out.

When we arrived, the school looked massive and there were kids everywhere, I stepped off the bus and felt like Bambi, my legs had all gone weak and I thought I was going to faint. Suddenly, this lovely girl came to my rescue and it was someone I knew from the village. Hurrah, I felt like hugging her and she must have seen the look of relief as she did give me a hug and reassured me that I would be OK. She took me under her wing and I thanked her for doing this, she really saved the day.

My first class was Maths, yuck! Not one of my favourite subjects however I sat next to a lovely girl - she was so confident and made me laugh. I instantly relaxed and thought everything is going to be OK.

Mum dressed me in this disgusting skirt and shoes which I hated, and I looked so frumpy compared to the other girls - but this was all we could afford at the time, so I carried on looking shit, in my eyes. A few years later I managed to save some pocket money and secretly buy myself a tight skirt. I loved it and felt I looked so trendy. I used to go as normal in frumpy wear when I left the house, say goodbye to mum then change in the garage to the new trendy skirt and then go to school; Mum never knew - naughty hey! I did however get too cocky and one day ripped the skirt on the side of the garage door, I was so gutted. I came clean and told Mum and I think she actually felt sorry for me and bought me another one!

I went through school in and out of a haze I think, as I can't remember lots about those days apart from the fact we used to have bundles down the aisle. When class changed that was great fun as I used to lift my feet off the ground and go with the flow. I got very bored at school and spent my life daydreaming or disrupting the class. I found school too regimented and I wanted to be free.

I am sure all of my teachers hated me and I remember one day I came in with all my new jewellery and make up on. I was summoned to the headmistress's office and she took one look at me and confiscated the lot; I didn't get my jewellery back until the end of term. I must admit, I used to spend a lot of time outside the headmistresses office, in detention or being reprimanded for talking or mucking about. My concentration levels were very poor although I did like French and found this really easy and sport. I used to love playing Netball and this became my favourite sport and I played for the school team.

I had two best mates and they were great although we did seem to fall out a lot and have shouting matches down the school stairs, goodness knows what the arguments were about, they felt very real at the time and sometimes we didn't speak again for days. I felt very much alone at school and never really fit into any groups or with the popular girls. I used to talk to everyone, but they all huddled in their own groups. I did used to get on with the boys surprisingly enough and actually preferred their company. I also used to get bullied and constantly called names like lanky streak of piss or fried eggs as I had no boobs. Horrible really, as this didn't help with my insecurity or confidence and made me withdraw even more.

Shock horror - I started smoking at 13! I used to walk up the alleyway behind our house in Bicknacre with our neighbours and pick up old butt ends and finish them off - how disgusting is that! But, I didn't care it tasted good. I also used to nick my mum's cigarettes when she wasn't looking out of her top drawer. I wonder if she knew - if she did, she never let on.

I always had an over active imagination and used to suffer really badly from nightmares, every opportunity I got to sleep in Kate's room I would. I was petrified of the dark and this may have stemmed from a film I watched when I was younger with the neighbours. It was called *'Nightmare on Elm Street'* and all I can say to anyone who is reading this do NOT watch this film. I have suffered for years with this memory and have spent many nights laying wide awake not wanting to sleep. I also used to feel an evil presence in my room, which sent shivers down my spine. I never saw anything but could sense something lurking in the dark. I used to hide under my covers, with the sweat dripping off my forehead and face, praying that I would be OK and protected. It was terrifying and I don't think Mum realised how bad it was. I used to spend nights crying myself to sleep but then the next day didn't say anything, so again kept it inside and put the thought to the back of my mind and pretended all was OK.

Kate started two years later at Anglo-European and I loved her being there. She was bullied at school too and I tried to stick up for her each time. I do remember once when this girl was being particularly nasty to her, I went straight up to this girl on the bus and slapped her round the face and said leave my sister alone or else! Everyone was in shock and I don't know what actually came over me. She left my sister alone after that, so I got the result I wanted, perhaps not in the best way though.

As it was a foreign exchange school we went on trip abroad and I will never forget when we had a swap over with France. A French girl came and stayed with us and she thought our house was a palace. She walked round and said she felt like a princess. I didn't even question at the time why she thought that but soon found out when I went to visit her house in France. Holy shit, I wasn't expecting quite what I was faced with there. I was super excited about going on the trip and was trying constantly to contain my excitement. The French student met me at the school and took me back to her farmhouse. Firstly, I was shocked at the lack of furniture, carpets and curtains in the farmhouse. There was literally no heating and the house smelt of rancid poo. I found out why this was later, the girl had 12 brothers and she was the only girl apart from her mother. There was no Dad, but a Grandfather who was the head of the family. I remember sitting there on my own at the end of this massive table with all the French family, they could hardly speak English and I felt so alone and scared. They were trying to include me but all I wanted to do was go home. Mum rang later and I burst into tears saying I wanted to come home, it was so daunting and I was completely out of my comfort zone. I must have been 14 but felt about 8. The smell was from the toilet and the Grandad used to go for a poo with the door open and stink the whole house out. It was a standing joke amongst the family of which I didn't find particularly funny. That first night I cried myself to sleep and just stared out of the window with no curtains into the vast field. I was in the middle of no-where far away from home and so frightened.

The next day I felt slightly better as was going to school to meet my other friends. I was greeted by the mum with no teeth and later found out she had put her teeth in my hot chocolate cup, nice! I did in the end really enjoy myself as I met loads of great French people and we had so much fun. I think after that initial night I took a deep breath and said to myself *'you are either going to sink or swim so you may as well get on with it.'*

I did a few more foreign exchanges with France and ended up with a French boyfriend, he was half the size of me with lovely freckles and a brace. I dated him for about 2 trips, if you can call it that back at school. We hardly went on a date but just hung out at school lunch breaks and after school.

As I said before, classes were boring although I nearly blew up the Chemistry lab by trying out an experiment in one of the lessons; I also tried to smoke a lint paper! Yeah right oh - gonna get a lot of nicotine out of that! NOT! Why I wanted or felt the need to do that I don't know. I was always being mischievous and trying to make people laugh. I hated homework although Mum, in order to help me with my exams, used to play games and list words on the doors and I had to go up the stairs one by one and remember the words or capital cities. I did learn loads this way and also Granny Toby was great in helping me with my Maths. She was a whizz at this subject and made it sound so easy!

Some weekends I carried on going to visit Dad and Lucy, and by then I had a half brother. He was a cutie and I did enjoy cuddling him. When I was 14, I remember having enough of going down to Dad's, and Mum said *'if you feel that strongly I suggest you speak to your father direct.'* So I rang him up and said I didn't want to come and see him anymore. He asked why and I said *'I hate that bitch you're married to.'* He then waffled on about that being no justification and some other bullshit so I put the phone down and didn't speak to him for 7 years - just like that. I had never forgiven him for leaving my mum and having the affairs in the first place. That was the last time I saw their son, my half brother and he was only 1 year old.

Out of school I used to spend a lot of time at the squash club as Mum used to work up there. I loved being there as it was full of men playing sport and I watched for hours. I got a crush on one of the boys there and used to swoon at him all the time. He must have thought what an idiot I was! I started having squash lessons with him and felt so nervous but secretly enjoyed it. His girlfriend used to watch from the balcony and send me evil daggers. I was no competition for her as she was gorgeous. I felt totally ugly next to her but could still dream. I am not going to tell you his name just in case he ever reads this book!

I also was really great friends with Jacqui; now she was amazing and super funny. We used to be in fits all the time and she had so much energy. We occasionally went to London to clubs and had a great laugh, mucking about with the boys. I must admit I started going to nightclubs at a really early age and used to spend nearly every month down at the local one called Dukes. It was brilliant and I loved dancing and the freedom. Mum was pretty relaxed and used to pick me up all the time. I remember going to Take That with Jacqui and we had such a laugh - I loved them, however, it was a close call with Adam Ant and Shakin Stevens too. I used to have them on my wall and would constantly try and super impose myself on photos as if I was actually with them! Weird hey!

School was where I met my first serious boyfriend, him and his friends used to hang round the school gates on their flash bikes waiting for us girlies to come out. I took a shine to one of them and we hit it off straight away. I was super impressed with him and was overjoyed when I found out he liked me. I had loads of insecurities, and this boosted my confidence no end. We used to go over to the park in Bicknacre and sat chatting for hours on the swing with his mates. I also used to spend a lot of time at his parents' house and I had started drinking then and smoking like it was going out of fashion. Back in those days you were still allowed to smoke inside which made all your clothes and hair stink. It was vile and totally gross but we still did it.

When mum was away we had a few friends round for a secret party without Mum's permission. My fella took me up to the bedroom and started kissing me, I knew where this was headed and thought I was prepared. Bearing in mind I was a virgin and didn't really know what on earth I was doing so I let him take the lead. He was extremely forceful and it was really hurting, I told him to stop but he carried on until he had done the business! I felt violated and empty it was the worst experience of my life, which was supposed to be the most special.

I never told anyone about that night as I was too embarrassed and felt degraded and used. I continued to smile and pretend everything was all OK, so again I put my emotions to the back of my mind and masked how I really felt inside.

Things went from bad to worse and my fella became very possessive, he wanted to control me all the time and we often were arguing about nothing. One night we were out down the pub and I was getting chatted up by this bloke and was enjoying the attention and flirting back, it was harmless banter. The next thing I knew my boyfriend was banging on the window for me to come outside so I stupidly went. Before I could say anything he punched me full pelt in the stomach, I fell to my knees and couldn't breathe, I thought I was going to die. He bent over me and said sorry then when I started to get back on my feet he started on me again! I was absolutely petrified of him and didn't tell a soul as was so worried he would beat me to a pulp.

I tried to break up with him one Christmas but that back fired. He head-butted me on the nose, BANG it really hurt and brought instant tears to my eyes. He screamed at me and said *'now do you still want to go out with me?'* I was crying and just pathetically said yes. I felt so trapped and spent my life walking round on eggshells wondering when he was going to strike next. I knew he was having sex with other girls and only found out when I overhead people laughing at school about the car rocking whilst he was inside it with another girl. What had my life turned into - I was a mess and just carried on drinking and smoking to take away the pain.

It took for us to have a major car accident before I finished with him. Driving back from the local night club, and he was drunk driving an escort. My sister, some friends and I should never in a million years have got in the car with him but we stupidly did. She was in the front on some-one's lap and we were in the back. Suddenly he lost control of the car and smashed (what felt like slow motion) straight into the lamp-post. My sister was catapulted through the windscreen and when she came back, she turned towards me and said that wasn't too bad and then all of a sudden, her face exploded and blood just started pouring out of her face. I will never forget her face it was horrific, it was like something out of a horror movie. She was crying and once we all got out of the car we were walking round in a trance. A taxi finally pulled over and we got a lift to the hospital. Kate had to have 25 stitches in her face and I felt totally to blame. I felt mortified as I never comforted her as I selfishly didn't want to get my new white top dirty with blood! How selfish is that? I have never forgiven myself, even to this day about that incident. I felt like it was my entire fault as I was the older sister and should never have stepped into that car and put Kate at risk. Mum saw the damage the next day when Kate came down the stairs. She took one look at her and ran out of the house screaming, she was in total shock and again, I felt totally to blame, I was absolutely devastated.

We took my boyfriend to court and it was all very messy, he of course denied it and Kate got a measly £3k of compensation which was nothing compared to her huge scar left on her face. I hated what he had done to me and also to my sister, as a family it took us ages to get over that incident and relationship.

3

The States

I was glad to see the back of school but pleased that I had studied for my exams, under duress I may add, but still managed to secure 8 O 'levels and walked straight into a job with Barclays. It obviously helped the fact that my mum worked there although my interview did go extremely well, if I don't mind saying so myself! Nothing like blowing one's trumpet, but someone has too. I also continued with my much-loved sport Netball. I absolutely thrived on it and got into the County Essex Team when I was 16 years old! What a great achievement, I was over the moon and felt so proud of myself. Mum used to spend all her weekends driving me to and from Netball matches bless her. I received great training from a club called Wanderers in Upminister, they were lovely girls and I made some great friends. I was actually introduced to them by the sports teacher at Anglo European who used to be my Number one fan!

At Barclays I started in the machine room, worked my way up to cashier and then eventually Personal Banker and yes I had to wear those ghastly peacock blue uniforms. I felt a complete prat walking down Chelmsford High Street as everyone knew I worked for Barclays and would stop me in the street and ask questions about their bank account. We had great fun at Barclays and the people were great. We all used to go round in a group and often go away for weekends in caravans and party the night away!

I had numerous boyfriends from 16-20 years of age and basically played the field. I didn't respect myself very much and had serious insecurity issues. Kate had nicknamed me *'Rocky Mountain'* because of my bump on my nose and I was painfully conscious of this and felt ugly. I had no boobs and felt like a man, hence the school comment of fried eggs and lanky streak of piss. It was bizarre for all that I thought I was ugly I still managed to pull and made it my mission when I went out to see how many boys I could pull in one night. It became a game to me and I enjoyed it immensely. I think looking back it was feeding my insecurities and making me feel like I was accepted and not a complete failure. I was overnight camping at an event one time and I met this boy, stupidly we shagged without protection and he didn't manage to *'pull out'* in time. It was strange as I felt this weird feeling over the next few weeks as if something had happened. My boobs also starting growing and I started to feel sick.

I kept this to myself and went off to get tests and the inevitable was there. I had to tell Mum that I was pregnant which was the worst thing. I didn't know how to tell her and knew that she would be disappointed. I plucked up the courage to tell her and I was correct she blamed herself, I felt awful and spent the next 2 weeks trying to tell her otherwise. I ended up having an abortion, please don't judge me when you read this as it was the only option at the time, it was a one night stand and I didn't know the boy and I couldn't support a baby and to be honest I didn't want to either. I could barely look after myself let alone commit to a baby. Kate took the news really badly and didn't agree with my decision, she turned against me and told her mate round the corner to where we lived. The next thing I knew, the whole neighbourhood found out, I was the talking stock of the village and I was so embarrassed. Mum went mad at Kate as this was our private business and told her to say that it was a false alarm. The abortion process was awful and the nurses looked at me in disgust. I felt like I had been violated again and sat crying in the bath afterwards, rocking back and forth wandering in bewilderment about what I had done, questioning myself as to whether I had made a mistake and if I would ever get over the loss. As normal I pushed all my emotions to the back of my mind and tried to pretend that everything was OK. The mask once again pulled over my true feelings.

For my 18th Birthday I was given the most beautiful gold Krugerand necklace from Mum and for the rest of the day I remained pissed somewhere in a local pub, so can't actually remember much of that day at all. Either that or I had a mental block and chose not to remember it. I did party a lot and went out with all sorts of sundry blokes. I used to spend a lot of time in Dukes, the main nightclub in Chelmsford, it was brilliant and the *'in'* place to be. When I had ran out of money, I went round drinking everyone else's drinks that had been left on the side. How disgusting is that, there is no way in this day and age you could do that now. I spent the majority of my time getting drunk and smoking and wasted a few years in total oblivion as to what was going on in the real world and with everyone in it. I suppose it was my way of dealing with the emotions and thoughts that were constantly going on in my head.

Now this is bizarre, so you know earlier on when I told you I had seen a guy in a building and I commented to my mum that I wanted him to be my Dad? Well spookily enough, he split up with his wife about 10 years later, then hooked up with my mum a few years after that. Can you believe it? Mum and Trev became an item and eventually we moved from Bicknacre to a gorgeous house in Hatfield Peverel. It was huge compared to where we had been living and it was in an ideal spot, right near to the train station. Things were extremely difficult at the start as Kate, Julie (Trevor's daughter) and I were all living in the same house. So you have a 19 year old, and two 17 year old females living together. I will leave it there as that is a story in itself and something I don't particularly want to dwell on.

I was still working at Barclays when I met my next boyfriend Dan one night in Dukes. Now he was fit and looked like a model. He was your typical tall dark and handsome fella and I was bowled over and totally hooked from the moment I set eyes on him. Hallelujah - he actually felt the same - I couldn't believe my luck. I still really lacked confidence and felt so overwhelmed when any bloke showed an interest in me. This relationship was mentally challenging, Dan used to test my love for him every weekend, it was most strange and I used to find it emotionally draining and very controlling. He was extremely possessive but rather than the physical element this was mental abuse.

He lived a distance away so we often travelled back and forth through the Dartford Tunnel. Kate started going out with his mate so she came with me, I must admit the four of us did have a great laugh when Dan was in a good mood. Dan had two cars, one blacked out windowed Sierra and a gorgeous black TVR, now that was amazing and I used to love him picking me up in the sports car. The noise it made sent ripples down my neck and I felt on top of the world when we drove in it. I do absolutely love cars especially fast sports ones, it was my dream at the time to have a Black Toyota T bar MR2 and no matter what, I was getting one within the next 5 years. BANG – I put it out in the universe to see how the magic works.

The recurring nightmare I had when I was younger - well Dan had a picture of the said person on the back of his door and I pleaded with him to remove this but he didn't, so every night I had my worst nightmare on the back of the door staring and watching me whilst I was in bed. I was so frightened and only felt safe when Dan cuddled me. Perhaps that is what he wanted so I became totally dependent on him for a short space of time, so serious mental abuse really. How I put up with it I don't know but I did for a long time.

I decided in this time to actually make contact with my Dad again, I had heard through the grapevine that he had an affair with his secretary who was 15 years younger and left Lucy in a right state. I know I shouldn't have thought it but I was secretly pleased that it had happened. Now Lucy would realise what she had done to my mum and us as a family. I know it takes two to tango but I still blamed Lucy for the majority of what happened. Dad had left another family and moved up North with his new girlfriend Sarah. I decided to meet him and Sarah in London with Dan, so we met on one of the docked boats along the Embankment. It was awkward at first but Sarah was really pleasant and I had no grudges with her so started to build the relationship back up with Dad.

On my 21st Birthday Dan used my razor and cut his face and blamed me as it was my razor. Mum had arranged a party for me at the house and invited lots of my friends. I was really looking forward to it but a dampener was put on it because of this incident. You could hardly notice his facial cut but he ignored me the whole time. It probably didn't help that I had two of my male friends there who I used to get on with really well; they were great and I loved spending time with them. Dan ignored them too and made me feel like shit. I was so conscious about him the whole time that I didn't enjoy the day. I tried to but he kept sending me daggers across the room. That is what I meant about mental games and torment. It really affected me and I was so upset.

At Barclays they were offering *'Special Leave'* which meant you could take up to 3 years off work and were guaranteed your job at the end of it. It was an amazing opportunity and one not to be missed, so I took a year off and Dan and I decided to go to the US to travel. We had been thinking about doing this for a while so had been saving up to support ourselves and then BANG this happened. Perfect timing me thinks! It took a while to arrange the visa but in no time at all we were off. It was a wrench when I left my family and had a few tears but we promised to keep in touch and Dan said he would look after me.

First stop was the Big Apple - wow what a place, jaw dropping in fact. In New York we stayed with Dan's aunt for 2 weeks then got a flight to Florida, stayed for a month in Fort Lauderdale, which was amazing. The heat was unbearable and so humid but we still loved it. Dan was extremely possessive and wouldn't allow me to talk to people but by then I had accepted it and just carried on enjoying myself. Was this normal behaviour - I never questioned it at the time. We bought a run-down car, which was full of cockroaches, yuck, they were like big black beetles and gave me the heebie jeebies. We hoovered it all out as best we could and then we were off, the world was our oyster as they say. We drove to Miami, all the way down the West coast to Key West, which was incredible. We spent some time in Disneyland, I got so excited with all the characters and really thought they were real. So gullible! I remember running up to Chewbacca and just giving him a big hug. I was 21 but felt like I was a little girl again; it was like fantasy-land and they had an amazing procession at the end with fireworks. My mouth remained open the whole time in total awe and amazement. One day I will treat all my family to go to Disney together and enjoy the experience as one. We continued our journey and stopped off at; New Orleans, New Mexico, Dallas – where we had to visit the place where they filmed Dallas, South folk ranch. It even had the cow that was in the series, how funny is that - I half wanted JR Ewing to turn up and say Hello. Tennessee had all the blues songs bursting outside into the street from inside the bars, which was incredible to hear. It was like being on one big film set and the roads were huge. We stopped at the Everglades and went on a speedboat and fed crocodiles marshmallows! It was surreal but fantastic.

I was living the dream and loved the Americans and they loved us. I kept being asked to talk as they love the English accent. We arrived in San Diego which is in California 3 weeks later and I fell in love with it straight away and thought I would definitely come back here one day. We drove up to Hollywood and I felt like Pretty Woman walking down Rodeo drive. I got so excited at seeing the hotel that was in the film - this is my favourite film of all time so I was taking pictures left, right and centre. We went to a bar called the Roxbury Café in Hollywood and this was apparently the place where all the famous stars hung out. I was super excited and wondered who we would meet. Whilst we were in the club there was a man beckoning me over to come into a private area. Dan cottoned on, and proceeded to tell me to stop flirting and encouraging the bloke. I wasn't even doing anything and if Dan had bothered to ask me I would have told him. I later found out that Prince had been in the private area so if Dan hadn't been so jealous we might have been able to see him. What a shame, I was really annoyed as it stopped me from doing something that I wanted to do. I just didn't have enough confidence to stand up to him, so shrank back into my shell again.

We left Hollywood and headed up to San Francisco, which was completely different but again jaw dropping. The Golden Gate Bridge and Alcatraz blew me away. Alcatraz for its eerie atmosphere and the feeling you get being in the prison and the bridge for its magnificent structure. There were trams everywhere and you had to be careful where you walked. We also took a trip out to Las Vegas; they call this the city that never sleeps - I have never ever experienced a place like it, it's like a completely different world and anything goes. Everywhere you look something is happening and the hotels are amazing. We watched the sunrise on the top of the Grand Canyon, I don't think I have ever experienced anything like it. It was absolutely breathtaking and something that I will remember forever. We also spent some time in Palm Springs and ironically saw Gary Glitter in the petrol station with no makeup on it was all very bizarre. It was here in California when things started to change with Dan. One day I said I didn't want to have sex at that moment in time as we had just come back from the beach but Dan took it as rejection and seemed to change from that day. He became really distant and was extremely nasty to me. I rang my mum and was crying down the phone saying I wanted to come home - it was awful. He had all the money so I didn't have any money to get a flight home. Mum sent me some money to feed myself as I think I said I would like to carry on and get a flight back from New York to see if things changed. I wanted to enjoy this trip so I put it to the back of my mind and put on a brave face. I was miles away from home and needed to rely on this man to help me so I remained calm and submissive and agreed with what he said just to keep the peace.

From California we drove across the National Parks through Colorado which was equally amazing, down to South Dakota where the Presidents are carved in the rocks and back through the middle of America. The only place we didn't manage to see was Chicago, the windy city, as this was at the top. We ended up back in New York and met a lovely bloke who took us to all the tourist places which was brilliant.

Not long after we got home I finished it with Dan, I couldn't handle the possessiveness it was unbearable and claustrophobic. I needed space and I was definitely not getting it in this relationship. He didn't seem that bothered and never rang me to try and get back together, so that was the end of that. It felt like a weight had been lifted off my shoulders and I felt free.

I had moved to Witham with work and was now an Account Executive at Barclays Premier, it all sounded really posh and we used to deal with clients that earned over a certain amount of money. We had a great team atmosphere and the managers there were a great laugh, mostly blokes I might add. I always seemed to have a better relationship with men than I did women. I found some women too cliquey and bitchy. This is where I met Clarice who was one of the managers and we hit it off straight away and along with Leona, one of the other Account Executives, we used to spend a lot of time together. Out and about for lunch and socialising out of work too.

I met James my next boyfriend not long after that, now he was great looking too and had a sort of gypsy look about him with long tousled hair. We met in a bar called Churchill's in Southend which was another *'in'* place to be at the time. I loved it there as it was just a constant party and everyone getting pissed! I spent a lot of time where James lived down in Hullbridge, his family were lovely and welcomed me in. We used to spend nearly every Sunday down at the Indian. I never used to like it before but soon became hooked!

About a year later, James and I decided to get a house and we moved to South Woodham, some-where in-between Hatfield Peverel and Hullbridge. We took the plunge and went onto the house owner's ladder, it was scary stuff but we did it. It was a cute two bedroomed property and I bought a ginger cat to go with it! I love my animals, we named him Tigger as he had ginger stripes and he was the most disobedient cat in the world and used to wee in the pot plants! Our relationship was very up and down and he used to smoke pot which I hated as it used to mong him out beyond words. We went up to visit Granny Peg one weekend and that is when it all fell apart.

4

Volatile

We had come to visit Granny Peggy in Wales but ended up staying in a hotel nearby and were due to see Gran the next day. That evening in the hotel bar we met two other couples and joined them playing cards and fun games whilst drinking. During the evening I was chatting to the bar maid who was pleasant enough and she commented on how good looking my boyfriend was. Now don't ask me why I said this but I replied by saying *'He is not my boyfriend he is my brother.'* She was taken back and seemed pleased and said she really fancied him so I said *'Go for it!'* In the back of mind I didn't entirely trust James so I thought this would be a test, which I know is wrong, but I wanted to see what would happen. When the opportunity came later for the group to get some food I jumped at the chance and ended up going to get some chips for everyone with the two guys from the group.

We must have been about 45 minutes and when I returned there was no sign of James or the bar maid and I immediately knew something had happened. Call it sixth sense, but I had a feeling of dread come over me and felt sick. I addressed the two girls calmly and asked *'Where's James?'* And they looked sheepish and said they didn't know. So I ran out the bar and headed for the toilet, there was no one in the men's toilet but in the ladies the cubicle door was closed. I slammed on the door screaming *'James I know you are in there'* which was followed by silence, so I kicked the door down and to no surprise they were both in there with James' trousers round his ankles. I went absolutely mental and then ran upstairs to the bedroom and flung myself sobbing on the bed. I don't know why I was so shocked as I knew that something was going to happen and I had instigated the whole thing. James was now banging on the door asking to come in so I mustered up all the strength and swung the door open and went to punch him in the face, calling him all the names under the sun. I wasn't interested in what he had to say and finally went to sleep crying with the keys under my pillow. My plan was to drive home on my own tomorrow and leave him to get back on his own. I felt empty as had always had my suspicions but didn't think he would actually do it whilst I was away with him, even if I had set him up. I felt like shit in the morning, like the energy had been zapped from my body, the keys had disappeared so James had obviously read my mind and nicked them back. We went to see Gran in silence and I put on a brave face and said Goodbye to her. We drove home in silence and when I got back I went straight round to mums and balled my eyes out. Surprisingly enough Mum was very diplomatic and said for me to wait until things calmed down and to try and make things work. So I did for the next 6 months but kept having flashbacks of that night, so ended it one day out of the blue when coming home from work. I left James with the house and everything in it. Why I don't know -perhaps I blamed myself for what happened and felt guilty, so yes he got everything and I returned to my mum's with nothing but the clothes on my back, ready to start all over again.

During my time with James I got a new job in London working as a Team supervisor looking after 22 staff. Wow, now that was hard work and I dealt with some very different and difficult personalities. Unfortunately when you are in charge of a team you can't be everyone's friend so I struggled initially to cope with the job. I did the best I could but always felt defeated. I did meet a lovely girl there called Caroline and my best friend Tracey was working as an Account Executive so that made it easier and we used to spend loads of time down the pub at lunchtime. A lot of wine was consumed whilst I was at Barclays and London was definitely the party city. I met Tracey back when I first started at Barclays and we hooked up pretty quickly and made really good friends. Caroline was completely different and was so scatty; she used to work out of a box and I was horrified when

I first arrived - we still laugh about it to this day. She was extremely good at her job though and helped me tremendously. She had to deal with all the managers and blimey she had her work cut out for her. At Christmas we all went out and had a great evening and that is where Tracey met her future husband, James which was all very romantic and totally set up like Cilla in blind date. I later became one of Tracey's bridesmaids, I had never worn a long dress before, and it was a first and was definitely a picture to be seen. It was a great day and her partner is a great guy, so I was very pleased for both of them.

Kate and I went to visit Granny Peg that summer as she had a fall, and we wanted to see if she was OK. It was great to see Gran again but we knew when we drove back that it would be the last time we would see her, call it intuition, as she passed away a few months later. We were so pleased we had made the effort to drive the distance to see her as it had meant a lot for both parties. Gran's funeral was held in North Wales and by this time Dad and his new girlfriend had a baby, which was my half sister. The baby spent the whole time crying during the funeral. I know that babies can't help it but Dad should have taken her outside as all I wanted to do was listen to the words of what was being said and pay my final respects to Gran. I was fuming with Dad but as normal he was oblivious, perhaps I should have said something but I was afraid of upsetting him so didn't bother.

I was still living at home whilst working in London and then I met George. He lived in Bicknacre, which was quite ironic considering that is where I grew up and the weird thing we never crossed paths. We met at Reds the local night club in Chelmsford, I had seen him about before and fancied him then and thought one day he is going to notice me. At that time he was obsessed with this other girl but I had clocked him so the intention was there and did think that one day I would go out with him. For some reason I'd been standing by the men's toilets and no this is not a normal occurrence, I just happened to be waiting for my sister who had gone to get something from the cloak room. George appeared out of the toilet and was facing me so I thought it's now or never, his hair was wet so I basically said *'What on earth have you done to your hair and what the fuck are you wearing around your waist?'* The belt was hideous! His mate wet himself and George just stood there and smirked and then walked off. I had obviously made an impression as about 30 minutes later he had hunted me down and asked me for a drink and that is where the romance blossomed.

He took me on my first date to Danbury Park with a picnic basket full of champagne and fruit and chocolates, it would have been perfect however I didn't like champagne and told him that straight away. Talk about bursting the bubble - who said romance was dead! I wasn't the most diplomatic person in the world however we still had a great date. George blew hot and cold and there were plenty of times when I left his parent's house after a debated argument or when he stormed off in a mood. His brother was great and a professional golfer, he was married at the time and they had daughters Maggie and Ellen, they were proper cute. We had some great family meals despite the volatile relationship between George and I. We moved to Chelmsford and lived right near the town centre which was perfect for me for going up to London as it was so near the station. The house was a lovely old Victorian place. We spent loads of time doing the house up and George worked really hard. He was a very controlling guy and I used to find that when we argued I started to become very submissive and withdrawn and would back down. George was 7 years older than me so I sometimes felt a bit intimidated, however we did used to have a great laugh and his personality was infectious. Unfortunately we both got into the drug scene and I was trying out a mixture of skunk and coke, which could be fatal. I must admit coke never used to affect me but skunk I loved as it made you find everything so hilarious and I mean everything. You just laughed constantly until the tears were streaming down your face. I didn't give it a thought though on how it would affect me mentally, you don't when you are in the midst of it. That is now something I regret getting involved in. I became obsessed with the gym and used to binge drink all the time; wine was my downfall and I used to drink about a bottle a night and some more if I fancied it. A dangerous slope to go down, as I became hooked - to the point that I used to pass out in bed, or be completely incoherent. I don't think George really knew the extent of it as I used to hide it and carry on as if everything was OK. It wasn't that I was unhappy, but George was extremely hard to live with and our relationship was very volatile. Everybody else thought we had the perfect relationship as on the outside we probably looked like we did, but no-one knows what goes on behind closed doors.

I am extremely family orientated and we used to have lots of family events, with my Aunts, Uncles, parents and Cousins. There were a few times that George, at the last minute, cried off so I ended up going on my own. I don't know why he had a problem with my family unless he was fighting his own demons. I used to get on really well with his Dad and we often had long conversations about the universe and that things happen for reasons. George introduced me to the book, The Celestine Prophecy and if you haven't read it I suggest you go and buy it. It's a fascinating book about how people come into your life for reasons and where this leads you to. It's so true and very thought provoking. His brother split up with his wife a few years later and started going out with Shirley, we hit it off like a house on fire and she was super funny and completely mad - pardon the pun. They used to come round for dinner a lot or vice versa and we had such a laugh. George also had some great friends who we used to spend time with too, especially with one of his best mates in London. His flat was amazing and he worked in the music business. I was always nervous around him as he had this amazing aura and I must admit I felt intimidated and didn't want to embarrass myself so kept quiet.

I was finding my job difficult due to the mixed personalities in the team so when I was head hunted I jumped at the chance. I was approached by a lady I used to work with at Barclays Premier in Witham, and she asked me to come for an interview for an Operations

Assistant at an internet publisher company. They were based in a porta-cabin as they were at the time having a three-storey building built.

I was over the moon when I was successful as wanted to leave London and work more locally, so this was an ideal opportunity. It was a bit daunting leaving Barclays after 13 years as it was like one big family and I had learnt a great deal in my time there. The training was fantastic at Barclays and they really looked after you as a company but it was the right time to go.

Working in a new company was exciting and the Managing Director was really down to earth and friendly. There were three of us in the Operations office and we did have a laugh. There was a group of us from work that also used to go out together with couples and I remember one night we called up some spirits. We had a glass and were mucking about with it on this home-made Ouija board, drinks were flowing and we were all having a laugh. All of a sudden I spoke to it and said *'Oh err should I be smoking?'* Automatically the glass went to *'No.'* For some reason I decided to sit down and speak to this spirit we had called up, so carried on the dialogue. *'Do you know anyone in the room?'* It spelt out my name! Fuck I thought, and for some reason immediately thought it was Granny Peg (who had died about 4 years earlier). I still didn't really believe it so I said *'What is the name of your husband?'* So it spelt out Vincent. Now bearing in mind the only person in the room who knew that name was me, it was pretty freaky and I know that it wasn't made up. I still didn't quite believe it so I asked *'Who is your son?'* And it spelt out my Dad's name. It suddenly hit me that it truly was my Gran so I burst into tears. It was the most unreal experience but true. All I could think of next was to say *'Are you happy?'* And it replied. *'Yes'.* That is all I really wanted to know, and then if by magic the spirit had gone and we then had what seemed like an evil/negative spirit as it was saying nasty things on the board. We tried to get rid of it but unfortunately as we were not experienced it may have remained. All I can say to anyone who is reading this, DO NOT dabble in the Ouija board as you do not know what you are messing with unless you are trained as a medium or spiritual teacher. Further on in my story I explain why.

Meanwhile back in the land of reality, the Managing director of the company was a bit of a practical joker and he loved winding people up so we decided to play a trick on one of the ladies there. We had it all set up and I was ready to deliver it in the next morning. I didn't realise the huge impact this was going to have on my life, if I had known the consequences of my actions to what happened next I would never have carried the joke through.

That day was probably the turning path when I changed personality and became this pathetic excuse for a person, even more so than normal. All 3 of us were in the small Operations office and I launched into the planned prank, it was going really well and the lady was totally hooked. How I managed to contain myself and keep a straight face I don't know but I did with great difficulty. Her reaction went just as the MD had expected, although he wasn't there to witness what happened next. When she realised that it was a wind up, World War 3 erupted. She exploded and went from 0-100 in a second. I am sure I saw steam coming out of her ears, anyway she completely stripped me down and it basically felt like my arse hole had been ripped from my body to put it bluntly but hopefully you get my gist. Saying how dare I humiliate her like that, who did I think I was? I didn't know what kind of mood she was in. It went on for what seemed like an eternity and I added fuel to the fire when I said *'Chill out'*, she then erupted again into another long verbal abuse.

The girl sitting next to me was shocked but didn't stick up for me even though she was part of it and she let me get the full force of it. I shrank into my shell and changed my personality from that day. I lost all my confidence in a split second and when I got home I burst into tears. She treated me differently after that and you could sense the atmosphere in the office. We eventually moved into the three storey building and I shared an office with her. She treated me like shit and when I did notes out to the company they had to go via her first, where she proceeded to write over them in red ink and highlight what I had done wrong like teachers do at school. I remember once saying to her *'Why do you treat me like you do, you can be a right bitch?'* And her response was *'I expect a high standard from my friends.'* I thought well that's a joke - if you treat your friends like this then I feel sorry for your enemies. I am sure she had her own issues but you never saw them.

Thankfully she got promoted and moved offices. I was promoted to office manager and got an assistant who was lovely. The lady was directly opposite me so I could still see her watching me, it was all very bizarre and I remember she commented once about how many times I went to the toilet! I thought to myself, have you got nothing better to do with your time to notice how many times I went to the bathroom! I think she was concerned for my health but I did used to drink a lot of water at the time so that might have had something to do with it. She made me complete a log to check the times I went - I mean seriously, is that the sort of control you need at work? It felt like I was being micro-managed constantly. However, I loved my job so I kept quiet and once again pretended all was well in my world. After about 2 years of being there, my sister joined the company, which I absolutely loved. She started in Sales and I was so proud when she got the job as prior to that she was doing hairdressing. She was brilliant at her job and we used to go out to events and recruit all the new candidates. We had double decker buses that were all decked out with computers and in the company colours and logo, they were fab and I looked after them. It was hard work as there was many a time when they had broken down or someone had clipped a wing or something. I also organized a charity end of season celebrity football match at Wembley, which was amazing and raised lots money via an auction for the local charity. As much as I loved my job, my female boss at the time just put a dampener on my day, if I think about it now she was a mental bully. The power of being promoted had gone to her head and she just wasn't a particularly nice person. Perhaps it was how I felt as we never really talked properly about what happened that fatal day when I played that joke on her. When I tried to talk about it she wasn't even interested in hearing my side of the story so I just kept quiet. She used to make me feel inferior and I was a changed person around her. I wonder if she really knew how I felt and if she realised the affect she had on me. She wasn't very popular, shame as we used to get on really well when we worked together at the bank.

I was drinking heavily at this point at home as was trying to block out what was happening at work, however George and I went on some amazing holidays. He won Top Sales Manager of the year consecutively for 4 years, so we ended up going to Costa Rica, Canada, Jordan, Dubai, Gleneagles in Scotland to name a few and we were treated like royalty. I met some great people and had such a great time.

One year we visited Greece, Lindos of all places which is a beautiful island with donkeys taking you up to the Acropolis, which if I went now I wouldn't go on them, poor things looked like they were on their last legs. Again I was drinking heavily, and one night we were walking home down the little side street when a couple passed us, we smiled and then for some reason the girl screamed out at me *'You fucking slag.'* Now I am not an aggressive person but something went off in my brain and I saw red, I ran without thinking bellowing back at her, *'who the fuck do you think you are?'* And just grabbed her hair so tightly she couldn't move. Her boyfriend tried to protect her and then before I knew it George and he were engaged in a full blown fight. There were fists flying everywhere and this girl was shrieking for me to get off her, which made me even more determined to hold on. I was fuming -how she dare call me that. Crash - I turned round and George had hit this guy so hard that he had fallen to the floor and hit his head on the pavement and was out cold. I let go of the girl and she crouched to her boyfriend's aid, what had just happened?

5
The First Episode

It was like it had happened all in slow motion and on a film set, as we rushed off and called for help and then went back to the apartment in what I think was shock. George was still not talking to me and blamed me for everything. For all we knew this bloke could be dead, what an awful thought. It was playing on my mind all the next day, but luckily we had some friends who we met by chance on holiday so they defused the situation a bit. I was still worried, although I need not have been, as when we were walking home that night from the beach, the same couple walked straight past us looking fine and completely oblivious to our existence. It was as if they didn't even know who we were so it was all very bizarre, however I was relieved that the guy was still alive. Phew!

I tried to put the work situation out of my head so on my 30th birthday I hired a limo to take me and 9 other girls to London for a party. Even though my boss was as she was, we still had some good times and I invited her and another girl from work to my birthday do and we had a great time in a place called Tiger Tiger in London. I must admit I used to spend a lot of time in that place whilst I worked up in London, it used to be my local haunt and a great pulling joint! It was an extremely boozy night and I had the worst hangover the next day but hey it's all part of the fun! Actually, the majority of my weekends consisted of hangovers and feeling like poo - I don't know why we put ourselves through it time after time. It couldn't have been good for our bodies, we just abused them, or I did at the time. We drank ourselves into oblivion, felt like death the next day then got back on it the following day or even the same night! Why oh why!

Kate and her partner Mark got engaged which was amazing news, however Kate didn't want Dad to give her away as she felt that Trevor had been around for more of her life and acted more like a father, so she had asked him to give her away. Kate still said Dad could come to the wedding but unfortunately Dad exploded and proceeded to send all our baby photos back to my Mum, which also included me. What had I done? It was my sisters' decision, however that obviously didn't matter. Kate and Dad had a massive argument and that was that, end of communication.

George and I were planning a trip of a lifetime to Sri Lanka and the Maldives and I was super excited. I thought this would be my dream holiday and I would get married, or George would ask me to marry him; it would be so romantic and I couldn't wait. I might have painted a bad picture of what went on in our relationship, but it wasn't all bad, just perhaps miscommunication. We did used to have some right laughs and George's banter was great. When we arrived in Sri Lanka it was pissing down and then proceeded to piss down for the next 3 days on and off. George had booked in Monsoon period and didn't realise, that was a good start! Although I got to ride on an elephant which was fab until the heavens opened, then I was wet with an umbrella on an elephant in the middle of what looked like a swimming pool!

Maldives was supposed to be the best place on earth, but when we arrived the island was infested with mosquito's, and it was a nightmare. It might have been the fact that there was a redundant mini golf course that had lots of pools of stale water, which was like a breeding ground for the insects. George was indifferent the whole holiday and I think we only slept together once so my dreams of a romantic holiday were shattered and I went home feeling utterly devastated. Coupled with being bullied at work, my life seemed totally shit so I spiralled into a depressed state, as I could think of no way out.

So after bawling my eyes out in the Doctors surgery with Kate at my side, after taking the Prozac I was prescribed under much duress and along with taking some time off work, I slowly started to feel more like myself again over the next couple of months and I was much happier in myself. My mood lifted and this was a great relief. I felt like the world had been lifted from my shoulders. My relationship ended with my boyfriend, which was a good thing as things weren't right, I got promoted at work and finally I had the nose job I had always wanted. I had wanted this done for years ever since I was younger and people bullied me about my huge nose. I used to get called Rocky Mountain and was so embarrassed. Some-one tripped me over at a Netball game and for some bizarre reason my hands never came out to help me when I fell, so BANG I fell on my nose. Wow now that really hurt and the blood squirted out everywhere. I had a crowd around me and I remember one girl saying she could see the bone. Like I needed to hear that, I didn't even know what day it was or my name. I was whisked off in the ambulance and had my nose repaired. I was not happy and couldn't breathe properly so claimed on my personal health insurance to have a new nose. This was the best thing I had ever done, my confidence increased and I felt on top of the world. For once I felt kind of pretty with my new nose! As they say every cloud has a silver lining and how true was that saying at this present time.

By Christmas I really was back to myself, and the words from the psychic I went to see stuck in my mind. There was going to be a massive change in my life around May time, what on earth could that be? I met this great guy called Ray and we hit it off like a house on fire, he was so chilled and relaxed which was great for me. He played the guitar in the bathroom of all places apparently the acoustics sounded better in there! I rented out a house with one of my close friends, Sarah. Everything was going great and we had a great laugh together. Life continued and it was a relief to be enjoying myself again.

I am a very excitable person anyhow, but I began to feel better and better and my confidence started to grow even more, I was finding I was just going up to people randomly in the street and striking up conversations with them mostly about spiritual topics.

It was like I knew what they were thinking.

One morning I got a phone call from Mum saying *'Where are you?'* I was supposed to be helping her out at a Boot Sale and I had completely forgotten and this was so unlike me as normally I was really organised. I quickly got ready and then rushed across to the Boot Sale. I couldn't concentrate on anything and kept frantically talking to everyone that was there. Mum looked a bit concerned but just thought it was me being the friendly Liz, I always was, even if a bit more hyper than normal.

It was strange but the people I approached knew what I was talking about so it felt fine, the trouble was I was getting so confident that my mind started racing and I began to experience manic thoughts that came from nowhere and I felt like my head was going to explode.

I felt a strong sense of being invincible and that I was the *'chosen one'*. I kept repeating that I was *'Jesus's sister'* and I was here to make the world a better place. I believed that Robbie Williams was my saviour! I didn't care what people thought and I was just saying exactly what was in my mind with no filter. It was all very bizarre, I had lost total rationalization and didn't know what was going on. I was talking about gathering my disciples together and doing great things. I was so supremely confident and everything felt wonderful and heightened. It felt like the world was in the palm of my hand and that everything I touched would turn to gold. If anyone has seen the Bridget Jones film, there is a part in there where she takes some drugs and then starts hallucinating and thinking everything is marvellous and dreamy. Well it felt like that but multiply it by a hundred. Then my thoughts turned to that I could stop a train with my magical powers but it would be OK as I would be resurrected. Looking from an outsiders' point of view something was seriously not right.

I was still going to work and one day I started to back chat the Managing Director and being very forceful and confident in a group meeting. He recognised something that he had seen before in one of his relatives and was extremely concerned. He rang my parents and they came to pick me up and took me to the doctors. By this time I was jumping up and down like a lunatic and saying things all mumble jumbled. I was having so many manic thoughts that I thought I was going totally mad but I couldn't stop them. I was running round the Doctors waiting room talking to anyone that would listen. I was saying to people that I had the power to arrange for them to meet with their favourite celebrity. Heaven knows what they thought. I remember I said to my mum, *'you are going to take me to a Mental hospital'* and she said *'darling I would never do that.'* I don't think she really knew what the hell was happening, seeing her daughter like this was frightening and completely out of the norm. I was then taken to see a Community Psychiatric Nurse, my stepfather who was brilliant, accompanied me and tried to calm me down but I had lost it big time, I couldn't keep still. I was screaming at them both, *'you are not listening to me'* frantically jumping up and down. It was horrendous and in the end they took me away in an ambulance to another place.

I didn't have a clue and thought I was going to Rydall High as in the Grease Film, strange but true. I was seated on my own in front of a panel of people, like an interview and they asked me loads of questions. Did I hear voices? What was I thinking? All I kept thinking was that any minute the bell would go and we could all run out of school. I also kept thinking it was near 7pm and Top of the Pops was going to start and I was going to miss it. These people started to annoy me as they kept questioning me. It felt like I had ants in my pants and my mind was doing overtime. I knew that I was about to save the world and these people were delaying me. I was right and they were wrong.

I was then transported to a room and people were coming in and out of the room, it was all extremely bizarre and I was thinking where am I and what are they all doing here? Then I saw them leading my mum away and she was crying. Noooooo, I thought don't take my mum away; I thought in my head *'don't leave me here mum I want to go with you.'* I felt helpless and didn't understand what was going on. I wanted to scream but nothing came out and I will never forget the look of utter concern and confusion on her face. I didn't have a clue where I was, everything was alien to me and I didn't know who these people were. The people wanted to give me tablets but I refused as I didn't know why they wanted to do this and I felt totally fine in my mind. They were persistent and in the end I took the cocktail of drugs that was given to me and passed out.

6

My New World

I woke up feeling groggy but still hyper; I was ready for a new day in this new world of mine. I still didn't really have a clue as to where I was, although knew I was in a secure place, and I started chatting to all the people like they were my long lost friends - merrily thinking this is a nice community - I was definitely still not right. Every morning/evening I queued up to take my medication, I didn't have a clue what they were giving me and did suffer some major side effects, which were ghastly. I had locked jaw, where my teeth felt clamped together and rolling eyes, I couldn't get my eyes to focus or come down from the top of my head. It was extremely scary and I panicked until the doctor came and injected me with an alternative medication to remove the effects. My friends and family were fantastic and they came to visit me every day offering their support and advice; I think then it suddenly dawned on me that I was in a hospital. When I initially arrived, I was diagnosed with Bipolar disorder and sectioned under the Mental Health Act. I don't think I really knew what that meant at the time, however I knew that I couldn't leave.

The staff in the hospital were brilliantly caring and understanding, and we often had chats to see how I was getting on. They encouraged me to take part in activities and group sessions to get me back to normality as I felt like my brain had been frazzled. I was in hospital for 4 weeks and this was the best place for me at the time, I'd become a danger to myself and had completely lost the plot. I would definitely have 100% jumped in front of a train believing I had the power to stop it and my life would be no more. I thank my lucky stars that my boss spotted the signs and that I was saved.

When I came to being discharged, my mood had severely dropped and I was feeling deflated, not wanting to do anything. Whether this was due to the vast amount of medication that I had taken over the last 4 weeks was debatable. I had lost my home, my car and my job was in jeopardy; I went to live with my parents at the age of 32 as I couldn't fend for myself. I lost the will to live and still wanted to jump in front of a train, not because I felt I could stop it this time and I was invincible, but because I was clinically depressed. I stopped eating and stayed in bed for 2 weeks staring at a tree in my parent's garden, unable to cry, wash or move; I had no emotion and felt nothing. My parents tried to encourage me constantly and every night my mum came up to my room and held my hand and promised me things would get better. She used to fight back the tears and remained strong the whole time. I didn't believe her when she said that I would be OK, I thought this was it, my life was over. It felt like a black cloak had been pulled over my head and everything was blank. I had no thoughts, it was the weirdest experience I had ever had. I would not want even my worse enemies to go through what I went through as the feeling is unexplainable. I am normally a size 12 and am 5ft 10, I went down to a size 6 and was painfully thin and my bones started to show.

Without the constant encouragement of my parents at the time goodness knows again what would have happened. They had to monitor me 24 hours a day and wouldn't let me out of the house under any exception. I eventually started to come downstairs and have cups of tea, which was a start, and I was smoking cigarettes like they were going out of fashion. I remember bursting into tears one time when I couldn't eat my meal, what was wrong with me? One day Trev and Mum went out only for a quick walk to the shops, whilst they were out I became extremely agitated and starting pacing around the kitchen. I picked up a knife and felt like I wanted to cut my wrists but something stopped me and I am not sure what, but the next minute the front door opened and my parents were back. The look of shock on their faces was horrific as I was holding the knife in my hands. Mum rushed over and calmly took the knife away. I think they felt awful for leaving me and didn't realise how vulnerable I still was. They didn't go out again together and remained a constant support. I hated being like this but nothing could change how I felt, believe me I am a very positive person and I tried everything in my power to get me back to normal but I just felt numb. After two months my mum managed to get me outside and to the shops for some fresh air and to walk about. I felt like a zombie and just wanted to go home and hide. It took me 10 months to start to feel kind of normal again but my brain still felt blank and I couldn't concentrate or hold a decent conversation.

During my euphoric state, before going into hospital, Ray who became my boyfriend, stuck by me during all the shit; hospital, depression, the works. Eventually when I became better, in November 2003, I moved in with him, then in January 2004 I went back to work again part time. Although officially work was really flexible and supportive, it felt like everyone was walking on eggshells every time they had to deal with me. The staff treated me like I was an alien, staring and didn't know what to say. Their attitude towards me had changed, I just ignored it and the worst thing was they had put someone else in my position which made me feel like crap and also given me a desk right outside my bosses office, which was degrading and made me feel like a naughty school girl. Cheers for that, I thought, what so that they can keep an eye on me? I wasn't a moron, I'd had a breakdown, you wouldn't be like that or treat someone different if they had broken their leg and been off for a few months to recover. I started to once again enjoy my job and then the bullying started again from the power woman and I thought sod this I am off.' I didn't want to go down that route again so I walked out of my job, without thinking of the consequences.

I got myself various jobs promoting new bars in Chelmsford, they didn't pay well but I did enjoy it. I was still drinking heavily and one night I got so drunk I ended up crashing round a friend's house. The trouble was that my phone had lost its battery and Ray had been ringing me all night. I went home the next day and when I walked into the front room the police were there. I acted like nothing was wrong and Ray was fuming and upset that I hadn't bothered to ring. He was obviously worried about me and thought something bad had happened which I totally understood but I wasn't bothered. I must admit I didn't treat Ray very well especially after what he had done for me. Not sure why, perhaps I was still confused as to what Bipolar was all about. No-one seemed to know what it was and I felt ashamed and just drank myself into oblivion along with drugs. I thought I was immune and it wouldn't happen again but hey presto - it did again in April 2004.

Things hadn't worked out with Ray however I had met someone else called Matt who could read the signs of a manic episode building up and was able to calm me down quite effectively. By this time, I lived in a one bedroomed flat in Chelmsford. I loved it here and this is probably what made me have another episode as I wasn't particularly looking after myself and still drinking like a fish. Going into the next episode, I thought I was super-important and I ordered two limos and wanted to take all my friends to the Ivy in London for dinner. I was going to just rock up and of course they would let me in as I was soon to be a royal! What was I thinking? I also thought I was on a beautiful deserted beach somewhere and I stripped off all my clothes and walked down to the water. Unfortunately, I was really in my flat in Chelmsford at the time and actually walked two storeys down the communal stairwell, NAKED! Luckily Matt turned up and was able to persuade me it had started raining on this gorgeous tropical beach so I'd better get inside again! This was another manic episode however I managed to remain out of hospital this time, thanks to my boyfriend's support although my job ended which was no surprise.

Whilst I was in the flat and to keep me company I bought a rabbit that shit everywhere, all over the flat were little brown balls of poo. I took that back after 1 month as it did my head in so I then decided to invest in a budgie. I kept letting it out as I felt sorry for it in a cage all the time, unfortunately there isn't much space in a flat and it kept hitting its head so I was not surprised to come home one day and find it on his back out cold. Animals did not suit the flat so I decided to move out and stay with my sister on a temporary basis until I decided what to do.

I had a pretty good CV and was able to get another job quickly, so by the end of September 2004, I had a great job as a PA to the MD of an Office Furniture company and my life was looking rosy. It was a really sociable company and we were always out doing things together. The thing is when you are Bipolar and life is going well you tend to forget you have the disorder. I kept forgetting to take my medication (I know I should get a smacked bum for that) and went back to my old ways, going out every weekend and living the high life. I thought I was going to be Queen Elizabeth III. Nothing like reaching for your goals hey! Inevitably, around May 2005 I relapsed again.

My sister was extremely supportive while I lived with her and it was through a very stressful time. I don't think she was really aware what was happening with me and I must admit I used to treat the house like it was my own and go out when I liked and come back when I liked. I was there for about 6 months and I think that was enough for Kate and Mark, her husband.

At work one day I completely lost the plot and told them I knew they talked about me behind my back but that I didn't care as the company was a load of shit anyway (nothing like speaking your mind hey, obviously had no filter!) By this time I was extremely hyper again, my psychiatrist actually came out to see me and I started talking in French to him (or so I thought) only problem is I have never spoken

French in my life and wouldn't know a *'comment allez vous'* from a kick up the arse. The fact that I was speaking complete gibberish didn't hold me back, I knew I could speak any language in the world so a bit of French wasn't a problem. I was convinced I had special powers again and thought I was Wonder woman. While this was going on, the psychiatrist (rightly so) had called the boys in blue and I was then handcuffed and put in the back of the police car for potentially being a danger to myself. I ended up back in hospital again, however, my step father and brother in law who had accompanied me at the time, had witnessed the staff dragging me to the floor and pinning me down whilst pulling my knickers to the side and injecting me with drugs. I thought at the time is this really necessary as I felt fine but the doctors were obviously seeing a completely different picture compared to what I was experiencing. I was definitely super manic so perhaps restraining me was their only option but in front of my family was rather harsh. I don't think my brother in law Mark or Trev have ever got over that. I think they were also shocked at the staff completing this right in the corridor so publicly.

I was made redundant from the furniture company shortly after coming out of hospital, after my outburst I wasn't exactly shocked by the news. I got a temporary job with the council and gradually started to get better and back on track. I was there for 3 months and found it so boring and regimented. I was constantly looking for another job and was praying something else would come up soon.

I stayed with Matt for quite some time and things were really going well. I found a job in London covering for maternity leave on a contract with the Army Cadet Force in early 2006. It was quite hilarious actually as it felt like things were going back in time. I was working for a Brigadier and I felt like saluting every time I bought him a cup of tea. We did have a laugh though and I really enjoyed myself and felt important again. Once again things were going really well, then spooky things started happening, it was like the computer was sending me secret messages or so I thought and my mind starting going off on tangents again. A couple of months later I had another episode. I don't remember much about it because of all the drugs they gave me that time but it was the worst episode I'd had so far. I became very paranoid and was convinced that I was being watched and that all my family was bugged. I didn't dare go to sleep because I knew that Freddy Kruger (from Nightmare on Elm Street) would come and get me. Of course not sleeping just made the paranoia and delusions worse and I even turned against my boyfriend. I also said that my best friend and I were lesbians and I was the sister of Jesus. Wow what a cocktail!

You guessed it – it was back to hospital for me however I managed to escape, don't ask me how and it was not for the first time either. I went straight to the police station to give a statement about my boyfriend and the horrific thing he was planning to do! The police at this stage were familiar with me and luckily didn't take any action against my boyfriend and took me back to hospital.

Unfortunately during that episode I missed one of my cousin's wedding and I was most upset as he had a black tie event so everyone was dressed up to the nines, apparently it was amazing. I also missed out on going to see Robbie Williams that year, my friends and I had bought tickets and planned limo travel to the concert but I was sectioned in hospital so missed out on both events, which was a huge shame.

When I was discharged from hospital I was summoned to London to see my boss at the Army Cadet Force. They told me extremely firmly they had decided NOT to renew my contract, I burst into tears as I really loved my job. They didn't say anything and just looked at me whilst I wiped my tears and walked out. Looking back, perhaps I should have appealed their decision or taken it further as they gave me a pathetic reason as to why they weren't renewing it. Deep down

I knew why, but how can you prove that it is to do with your mental health? This is a prime example of stigma and discrimination in the workplace.

I went to visit Dad and his girlfriend to find out why he had done what he did years back over Kate's wedding and also to explain about my breakdown. I give them their due respect, as they did sit and listen for about an hour to me talking about my Bipolar. Dad also apologised for his behaviour previously, and said he just saw red and also included me when sending back the baby photos. I did try and get him to come down to Chelmsford to see Kate again but unfortunately that never happened which was, and still is, a shame.

I was offered lots of places to go for help and I did some volunteering at the local British Cross; this all helped with me getting back into full time work. The good thing is, that I was always in work or got paid so I never claimed benefits. I just am not that kind of person, to do nothing and not work - I would get bored!

It didn't take me long to find another job as I am one of these people that bounces back time and time again. I managed to get a job at a Financial Services company in the city. I finished with Matt as things weren't working out and bought a one bedroomed property in Boreham. I loved my little house and decorated it just how I wanted it to be. I had sundry fellas but none of any relevance, and then went on a date with a guy who I knew from round about Chelmsford. We hit it off straight away and started seeing each other virtually every night. I moved in his flat not long after I met him and rented my house out. I was still working in London at the same firm and used to party a lot up there. London is definitely a party city and I often used to tell my boyfriend that I would be home at 7pm and didn't arrive until 11pm, pissed and in a right state. I think I had a self-destruct button and definitely had a drink problem. I just didn't know my limit and my partner was only trying to look after me.

I however, felt like he was trying to control me and I became worse. He knew about my condition so was aware, but I had been OK for 2 years; so when the next episode happened I think it shocked the life out of him. It was October 2008 and things started to go pear shaped again. I was worried about my sister as she wasn't very well and I wasn't sleeping properly.

I felt like there was a lot of negative energy around me, and I started to have the weird spiritual feelings again. I kept talking about all things opposite i.e. black and white, good and bad, angels and demons. Panic attacks took hold of me so I decided to go and stay at my sisters where I felt safe. I still didn't manage to get any sleep that first night which is not a good sign and felt like evil energy was surrounding me. I then started to have manic negative thoughts. I remember pacing in front of my boyfriend at the time and Mark (my brother in law) telling them that I could hurt my nieces if I wanted to but I wouldn't because I loved them. What an awful thing to say but I obviously wasn't in the right mind again. It was like I was pre-warning them what could happen if I flipped. I had a rough night and the next morning I flipped and turned on my sister. I accused her of being a murderer and was pushing her aggressively and screaming at her. I ran out of the house and continued to scream, *'call the police!'* Heaven knows what people thought, but again, I had lost the plot.

I arrived at a nearby Tesco's and was begging the staff to lock the doors to stop *'them'* getting me and then I switched tone completely and started telling everyone it would be OK because Robbie Williams was my saviour and he would come and rescue me! A woman pushed past me and I flipped again and accused this woman's child of being the devil's child. Her partner was not happy and grabbed me in a head lock as I was going wild. The police arrived and were fantastic and did a great job of calming me down as I was all over the place.

My boyfriend got into the car alongside me, he just looked shell-shocked, he couldn't speak and I don't think knew what the hell was going on.

They rushed me to the hospital in Broomfield and I had to wait four hours to be seen by a panel of three doctors. The two police officers stayed with me the whole time just to keep an eye on me as at that point there was not sufficient hospital staff to sit and wait for the assessors.

The doctors assessed me, asking the usual questions which instantly got my back up. I began challenging them, asking them if they had seen my file (by now about 3 inches thick!) or knew anything about my condition. It was clear that they didn't know anything about me and when I realized one of them was actually falling asleep I lost it completely. I clicked my fingers and told him to *'wake up and pay attention'* as I was the important one round here! Again I was manic and the doctors had to calm me down, they injected me again with a cocktail of drugs and put me in the hospital ward with other patients for the night. I was absolutely paranoid and felt the negative energy again along with my worst nightmare. I literally kept going back to the nurses saying I needed help but this time they were not particularly nice or helpful. They kept sending me back to my room but I was completely petrified. I was not staying and I was in a room on the ground floor. I tried one of the windows and was surprised to find it open fully (they usually have restricted access and only open a little to allow fresh air in) so I climbed out and then walked towards home across the fields in my flip flops. Bearing in mind this was November, you would think someone might think that was a bit odd especially as I was heavily sedated from the drugs they gave me, but even when I stopped at a pub (ironically called *'The Angel'*) for a drink of water, no-one asked me if I was alright or asked me what I was doing.

I found my way to a friend's house and Nick luckily was home. He took one look at me and put his arms around me and cuddled me. He got me inside and laid me down to sleep. He knew about my condition but had never witnessed an episode before. When I asked him later why he had hugged me (not normally something he would have done) he said I just looked so vulnerable that it was instinctive for him to protect me. Nick – you are a lovely man!

Not long after I had settled down the police arrived and took me back to hospital. I remained in hospital for about 5 days to recover. I didn't realise at the time that it was a secure unit where people with extremely dangerous and serious illness were housed. I was kept a very close eye on whilst in here by the hospital staff. My boyfriend at the time couldn't cope with my illness it was just too much for him so, along with some other reasons we ended up splitting up which was a shame but I think it was just lack of understanding, or perhaps it was sheer fright of what was happening. I remember getting a text saying that all my things had been moved into storage, I was totally gob-smacked and this caused me to have a massive panic attack whilst driving. Luckily my friend Bev was around at the time and managed to calm me down. I owe a lot to Bev.

7
Why Does This Keep Happening?

I moved in to Bev's house, as my one bedroomed house was still being rented out so I couldn't go back there due to the contract. My family had been advised from the Doctors to stay away whilst I was in episode for safety reasons as I was unpredictable. Now whether that was the right advice is debatable, as for me, it made things worse because I felt so alone. This was probably the worst time for me although Bev did her best to cheer me up and involve me in things.

I tried to pretend everything was OK but spent the next month like a robot, going to work and coming back to Bev's. My mood had slumped again and Christmas was looming. On Christmas Eve I briefly went round to Mum's and collected my presents and left, it was all very strange and I felt like I didn't belong. They must have thought I was acting indifferent but never stopped to question me, I think I probably came across as aggressive and moody. This was the first year that I spent Christmas away from my family and I was heartbroken. Bev went out with her friends that evening as I stayed in. When she departed I felt like my world had drawn in, I felt totally helpless and alone so I called my Dad to have a chat. I actually told him that I was planning to end my life and do you know what his words were? *'Is your Mother not about?'* SORRY WHAT I thought! I wanted to scream at him *'did you actually hear what I just said to you?'* I was utterly astonished so slammed the phone down. He didn't ring back so it just shows you what a complete dickhead he is.

My mobile rang a couple of seconds later and it was Bev asking me to join them down the pub, I was so relieved and jumped at the chance. I got ready in 5 minutes and went to the local bar in Chelmsford. You know the saying - things happen for a reason? Well

Bev's phone call saved my life that night. She probably doesn't realise to what extent, but I was not in my right frame of mind to be left alone, so was extremely grateful to her.

Whilst I was waiting for Bev at the bar, an absolutely stunning looking bloke was also at the bar, wow my breath was taken away so I decided to approach him, my cheeky side coming out. We hit it off straight away and he was an actor from London. Bev arrived with her friends and we proceeded to all have a great laugh. I met him a couple of times for lunch after that but I was still slightly in episode and there were a few strange incidents so I think I scared him off! Shame as he definitely had potential! My London job at a credit rating company was OK although I didn't have a clue what the business was all about. They seemed to speak in a foreign language to me although my boss was pretty cool. He cracked me up as he was so gay, and used to have botox in his bum! They were a good crowd at work and we used to go out on a lot of social events.

I eventually moved out of Bev's as I think I overstayed my welcome although she never said, things with my family were still a bit tense but we'd had a few chats to smooth the path a little bit.

One of my other friends Karen had a spare room at her house so I moved into there, during that time I met Darell a guy who I had known years before. We had a coffee and started seeing each other. Within about 2 months he had offered me a room in his flat and for no rent! I couldn't believe it - he was so generous and just wanted to help me. It was working perfectly as his flat was in Chelmsford and I walked to the station to get to my job in London. The weird thing is, Darell and I were more fuck buddies (excuse the French!) than boyfriend and girlfriend so it was a bit of an odd relationship, however, we still went to Cuba together for a quick break to help me get over my previous boyfriend. I wasn't much company but Darell was really supportive. When we came back from Cuba, I decided that Darell and I weren't going anywhere so finished the FB relationship.

I met a guy down a local bar in Chelmsford and he had a great sense of humour, we used to go to the same secondary school and he was the year above but didn't remember me. We started seeing each other, much to Darell's annoyance, and looking back I was really out of order, but I think I was still on the rebound from my previous boyfriend who had basically destroyed my world. That lasted all of 3 months and after coming back from Portugal with this guy I decided that I did want to be with Darell. He had been working out at the gym and I must admit was looking pretty fit. We got rid of the flat and moved into my property in Boreham to make a go of it. To celebrate I bought a cat called Bob Bobs, he was adorable with long black hair. Considering the house was so small we did get on remarkably well, however Darell did drink a lot and I wasn't sure whether I could cope with it as he seemed to be still in a boyish party mode, and every Friday he was down the pub.

Throughout these years I had some excellent training. I went to some Cognitive Behavioural Therapy courses and had regular counselling sessions. My psychiatrist was brilliant, so calm and always listened to what I said. He knew when I was manic and adjusted my medication accordingly. He re-emphasised the fact that I was to drink in moderation and change my lifestyle as he didn't want another episode to occur. He said to keep stress free and don't take on too much; some very good and worthy advice. I adhered to this and cut out alcohol and cigarettes altogether, I also started to eat more healthily and generally take care of myself more.

I had been clear of an episode for about 2 years and then out of the blue I had another episode and for a period of 2 weeks I felt really agitated and Darell was really annoying me. I woke up one night and thought I was Neo out of the Matrix; I was fighting some invisible beings and Darell didn't know what on earth was going on. I had prepared him for my manic episodes but he was still shocked. I picked up my perfume from the sideboard, which happened to be called Alien and we had to give the Alien perfume bottle back to the Alien King. In my mind it was an alien baby and was perfectly normal to be giving it back to its parents. Darell went along with it as I don't think he knew how to react.

I ended up in hospital again and I felt the same old negative energy/spirits around me, I was so bad and caused mayhem in the hospital, I thought that the Doctors were poisoning the patients so grabbed one by the throat and threatened him. Two big security guards dragged me off and took me to another ward where I was injected again. I was left in a room on my own in the dark, I wasn't sure what the hell was going on, and surely this was not right. I felt evil energy round me and I was hallucinating, I kept seeing witches in the window of the door and I was petrified. Eventually a Doctor came and put me to bed, I was out cold for 2 days! This apparently was medication to give my mind a rest, I was in the secure unit again and the nurses again were brilliant. The events from last night I had forgotten. They looked after me and we had long chats to check I was OK. My Mum and Darell came in to see me on a regular basis and it took me a week to recover. I remember once Mum spent an hour just brushing my hair which had become so matted where I hadn't bothered washing it. I was also back smoking again like a chimney.

I am not sure where the last episode came from as I wasn't drinking however I still needed to calm down and my Psychiatrist put me on a different medication which suited me better. My work-place, were absolutely brilliant, and so was my boss. I took a month off and they supported me big time. I had been honest with them from the beginning and advised them of my Bipolar, so my boss was aware and wanted to give me a chance. He left not long after that and I had a new boss who was great too. I did find the work tedious, but I loved the people. I stayed for about another year and then I decided to have a complete career change and try something different, which I had never done before.

I went to work in Social care, dealing with adults with learning difficulties. My friend Caroline who I worked with at Barclays worked there and suggested it to me and thought I would be a great carer. So I had an interview and started work there within a month. Darell was so supportive and he was excellent, bearing in mind I had literally cut my salary by more than half. I earned £8 per hour, which for that type of work is rubbish. If I had it my way I would triple carer's salaries as well as the people who work in the NHS. I was also relieved that I had at last found someone who was strong enough to cope with me and understand the nature of Bipolar.

Darell and I went to Antigua for his 40th birthday and me being me, I decided one night after a few holiday bevvies to grab the microphone from the rep and express my love for Darell by proposing to him. It wasn't even a leap year and when I did it Darell's' chin hit the floor and he was speechless. He did eventually come back to life and say yes but I personally think he is still in shock as I said at the time you need to ask me back and I am still waiting! It's now 10 years down the line! Who said romance was dead? We met some great people who funnily enough lived in Wickford and we are still friends with them now.

I started to do more exercise and go for jogs and still avoided going to the pub and generally started getting involved in different activities. The trouble is, in the back of my mind, I always thought that there was something more to the Bipolar condition that just a chemical imbalance, and being around upsetting behaviour whilst growing up. I am a very spiritual person and I asked for an Advance Decision to be set up between the doctors and me so I could state how I wanted to be treated prior to being admitted to hospital. I felt that some staff were not listening to me and just fed me medication to calm me down. I wanted to speak to someone who understood the spiritual side like a spiritual doctor or a church member. My Psychiatrist put me in touch with the chaplain lady attached to the hospital which really helped and I got the Advance Decision set up which made me feel more in control.

I passed my NVQ's in Social Care and I must admit it was one of the hardest and challenging job's I have ever had to do. The girls I worked with were amazing and so were the people we looked after. I decided to leave there after a year as it just wasn't for me, and I take my hat off to people who do those jobs. I went to work back in London as a Personal assistant for Barclays. I had managed to stay well for a year, however you guessed it, I felt the spiritual/energy connection again and started to become very excitable. I felt positive energy around me and I wanted again to help the world (not a bad thing I suppose)! I thought *'right this time, let's try and control it before it gets out of hand.'* I went to see my Psychiatrist and he said that he thought I was going high again therefore he put me on loads of medication again and said to take it easy.

It takes a while for the medication to kick in and I ended up spending £4,000 on my credit card or should I say Darell's' card as by mistake I used his!! Whoops!

I wanted to set up my own spiritual business. I was arranging business cards, setting up articles in a magazine and getting t-shirts made. Then, the medication started to kick in and I started to go down, I lost my temporary job at Barclays and spent the next few weeks feeling all doom and gloom. Darell again was brilliant and he encouraged me to get a new job and didn't stop caring or supporting me. I got a job working for the NHS in Wickford and loved it. This was a temporary contract, which lasted for about 3 months, as then I went for an interview and got an even better job; working as a Personal Assistant for an insurance company. I loved this job and had a very understanding employer and supportive colleagues. I informed the company about my bipolar condition and they were brilliant. They wrote to my doctor to get a report and all was fine.

I have had discrimination in the past from employers, I disclosed in one of my interviews that I was Bipolar, prior to that she loved me and said that I would really fit into the business. She said one of her friends had Bipolar so it wouldn't be a problem. I came away from the interview feeling really positive; a week later, they called to say they were not going to offer me the job as they felt it would be too stressful. I felt so annoyed and betrayed and I tried to ring her up, but alas, no response. There have been a few other examples, because unfortunately, many people don't fully understand the condition and there is still a lot of ignorance about it- HUGE ignorance in fact.

Although my new firm knew about my condition, my direct boss didn't so I felt it was the right time to let her know as I had been working there for about 3 months so had built up some trust and had also just been made permanent. I was so nervous when I approached her and I sat down with a serious look on my face. She had a look on her face as if to say what on earth is wrong with you. I blurted out that I had Bipolar and do you know what she said? I still laugh to this day - she said *'you looked so serious I thought you were going to say that you used to be a man'* - we did laugh! This made me feel much better as she then followed on to say that I was still the same person and my diagnosis of Bipolar didn't make any difference. How refreshing is that - compared to other people I had previously come across. I was over the moon and felt so much more relaxed in my job, it was a great feeling to be accepted.

We decided to rent the Boreham house out to a neighbour's friend who turned out to be a complete nightmare tenant and caused me a ridiculous amount of stress. It seemed like every weekend we were called because an incident had happened where the police were involved. I was constantly chasing my rent payment and when I took the flat back, they had trashed my house. There was blood up the walls, the carpet was heavily stained and the cupboard doors were smashed along with lots of other things. I burst into tears and slumped on the floor. My house looked like a total mess. Darell came to my rescue and said he would sort it all out and he did. He totally repainted it, repaired it and made it liveable again - what a diamond. We chose to move to Witham and sold the house in Boreham to a friend's parents who loved it. We bought a two bedroomed place and I felt at home as soon as I walked through the doors although Darell had to be convinced. I was telling him to visualise what it could look like and with his handy work and experience we could turn into a lovely home. We moved in within two months, which is pretty quick in the grand scheme of things, also I don't think we would of worked out if we had stayed in Boreham. Darell needed something else to focus on rather than the pub. A day after we had moved in, the place looked a shambles. Darell had started ripping cupboards out and demolishing things! It was pretty hilarious and I didn't care as I knew he was perfectly capable of turning it into an ideal house.

Darell had always wanted a dog, so for a surprise I bought him a puppy. My friends at work thought I was completely bonkers and tried to persuade me not to, however once I have got my mind set on something I carry it through. When he came home, he sensed something and talk about psychic he said straight away, *'you have bought a dog and you can fucking take that back now!'* Oh shit! But when he came in and saw the little puppy on the sofa, he melted and it was love at first sight. We named the puppy Boris - not after Boris Johnson but just because he looked like a Boris - he was a springer spaniel and our little baby.

I was also getting on better with my family so I often had my nieces who had now grown up, over to stay. We had great laughs dancing around the lounge and were lucky enough to have a hot tub in the back garden, so spent hours just relaxing in there.

I contacted Dad again even though I had put the phone down a few years back. We texted and again it turned bad. I remember vividly saying *'I am going to be writing a book about my life'* and the cheeky sod had the audacity to say *'Don't make me laugh, you write a book, as if!'* I thought at the time *'I will show you, I can and I will'* Funny how things turn out - who's laughing now hey?

Meanwhile, I started to conduct talks about Mental Health outside of work, for the NHS, in schools and at events. I wanted to educate people about this, as I didn't think there was much media coverage on Psychosis. I did a lot of research on different people's opinions of Bipolar. In the Western world we are very closed to the possibility of spiritual awakenings, however I know what happened to me and what I had seen and felt, so knew there was something more to it. I discovered that abroad, people called Yogi's can evoke their spirit and absorb other spirits or energies. I found all this fascinating but knew people would think I had totally lost the plot if I told them what I thought so I kept everything to myself. Darell and my family knew what my opinion was but I kept a lot of it under wraps. This was not the time to share my opinion of what my thoughts were on what could potentially happen to the mind.

All seemed to be going swimmingly well and 3 years had passed and NO Episodes, however sometimes things are just too good to be true. I'd been stressed at work and had taken a lot of extra work on when it started to happen again.

8
Dark Energies

So here I was again…

I started to get the all too familiar weird spiritual and sixth sense feelings but this time they became stronger and more intense. I remember thinking *'right what did my Psychiatrist say?'* I knew that Olanzapine would take a while to get into my system so as an alternative I took Lorazepam (which is a benzodiazepine or strong sedative) this knocked me out and as a result I had two excellent nights' sleep. On the third night, I was feeling physically ill, and also had the terrifying feeling of negative energy around me. I was unwell (sickness) and as a result did not sleep most of the night. Darell was unaware of my disturbed sleep as he was himself very tired. In hindsight I should have woken him but instead I started to panic with my mind racing all over the place. My mind was flitting from having cancer with a brain tumor to thinking the world was going to end. I had lost of lot of weight over the last month, nearly a stone and I couldn't really afford to do this as I am skinny anyhow, and I looked like a bag of bones.

The next day I decided to take the day off work and get myself down the Doctors, Darell came with me as support, bless him. They checked my bloods and thought it maybe my thyroid. I was very agitated and Darell could see that I was not myself, I was talking about the demons again so this raised alarm bells with Darell so we decided to ring my Psychiatrist. We left a message saying it was important for him to ring us back as I could feel another episode coming on and I didn't know what to do. I was starting to think all sorts of things positive and negative and was becoming paranoid that someone was trying to get me (this is all part of a psychotic episode). Paranoia is one of the worst things to experience, I could feel overpowering evil energies around me and was having increasingly evil negative thoughts which is so unlike me as normally I am very positive.

As we hadn't heard from my Psychiatrist we decided to ring the Crisis team. Darell spoke to them initially and explained to them that he was very worried and asked what he should do. They were completely unhelpful, to the point I even said *'well what happens if I thought aliens were on the planet'* their reply was laughable and suggested a lot of people think that. HELLO, I was crying out for help and no one was listening. The Crisis Team confirmed that as I was not having thoughts of self-harm or ending my life this did not constitute as a crisis. I knew I was going to have an episode but they didn't seem to take it on board, which was extremely worrying. I could not relax and had rushing manic thoughts raging through my head. My Psychiatrist's secretary who is very professional and good at her job rang us back and we booked an appointment for the following day. I was pleased about this and consequently my mind relaxed a bit.

Darell suggested we get away from the house as I was feeling increasingly claustrophobic so we decided to take Boris and go camping for the night, as the weather was lovely. In hindsight this was probably the worst thing we could have done, I was becoming extremely elated and the energies were everywhere. My brain was rapidly switching between good and evil, like some invisible being was playing tricks on my mind. I was seeing faces in the clouds again like I always do but they were more malignant. As soon as we arrived at the camp site I froze, something was telling me there was a lot of negativity around this place and I could sense evil dark energies, I immediately said to Darell *'I don't want to stay here lets go'* but he said *'we are here now so come on relax'*.

We met some really nice girls. Now for some reason, whenever I have an episode I go into film mode, so this is exactly what happened. I thought I was on a film (Like the Truman Show) and being filmed so I started to act out scenes from different films, goodness knows what the girls thought. I then started to get agitated and annoy Darell, I don't know why. We went for a walk and that's when bad things started to happen, I was imagining all sorts of strange things in my mind - that there were UFOs in the sky and that I was trying to shoot them down. The weird thing is I could actually see them in the sky and I was asking Darell to look but he was denying all knowledge saying there was nothing there. I was becoming more panicky and it felt like the whole planet was closing in on me, I started to distance myself from Darell and when I turned round to look back. Darell had turned into a ghostly spirit. I screamed his name and asked him to stop but he kept coming towards me. It felt like I was in a horror film, so I started running. I glanced back at one point and the ghostly spirit had turned into something with long hair and no face. I was petrified beyond belief as this was like my worst nightmare but I was awake and this was real life. It was probably one of the scariest things I have ever seen and I wanted to get as far away as possible from whatever it was. I ran and ran and ended up in the middle of the road and tried to wave a car down that was coming round the corner as by this time I was hysterical. As the car came towards me, I felt myself being thrown into a muddy ditch and Darell was shouting at me to stay down and acting like a soldier, it was all very bizarre. I felt like I was in a war zone and didn't know what was going on. When Darell had chucked me into the ditch it felt like something had popped out of my body and it brought me back to reality with a real bump.

Darell had, during the course of this entire episode, contacted the Police and my parents and the Police suddenly arrived out of nowhere. I was relieved however they handcuffed me, not sure why but hey I was so happy to see them as believe me when you see your loved one like that, you would go with anyone just to get away. I was absolutely scared stiff.

The police officers were brilliant, a bit abrupt at first but they did try and calm me down. The Police took me to the hospital near the camp site. I felt very panicky and initially refused to enter the building. The Police Officers were very patient and persuasive and eventually I was left with the nurses at the hospital and where I began to feel safer. I know that sounds strange as I was in a *'Mental Hospital'* but I didn't want to be outside in the world where I felt so susceptible to the negative and evil energy that had just engulfed me. I was thoroughly interrogated but responded reasonably calmly, a cup of tea certainly helped.

The staff in hospital initially read my rights and indicated why I was being sectioned. I started getting agitated again and asked for my Advance Decision, the arrangement that had been set up between my Psychiatrist and I which detailed what should happen in the event I became manic and in episode but unfortunately their copy wasn't signed or up to date so could not be used.

As they spoke to me, the negativity started again - feeling evil energy, and I started to panic and pretend that I needed to act out my worst nightmare so that I could release the demon inside me (all sounds very bizarre but to me it was like living hell). I started screaming for the demons to get off me and acted as it I was ripping something out of me. It was absolutely horrific but I felt I must show them that I had to release what was holding on to my mind and what I was convinced was a demon. I understand that in the Catholic Church, exorcisms are performed where specialist people perform this act. I thought I needed help from someone who understood spiritual encounters but I think the staff were totally shocked and I am sure I scared the hell out of them. I dread to think what it looked like if someone had filmed it, as I had totally lost the plot. Like one of the scary horror films that plagued my nightmares no doubt!

As a result of this I was persuaded to take a couple of tablets to calm me down and was then left in a room on my own to *'cool off.'* I hated it, and thought they were watching me and whispering behind the doors. My paranoia nearly hit the roof and I was totally out of control, as though my body had a mind of its own, and then 6 medical staff came in, held me down and injected me three times in the bum. Terrified and not wanting this to happen - I kept saying *'why are you doing this, I am only a human being, nothing to be scared of.'* After this, I was taken back into the assessment room and persuaded to take another two tablets. My mind was totally frazzled by then, my deluded paranoid thoughts all over the place and I thought they were trying to kill me. My mind was obviously over-reacting enormously. I remember one nurse said *'Trust us this will really help'* so I did what he said and swallowed the last two remaining tablets.

BANG darkness! That was it, the next thing I knew I was waking up in an unknown bed. I didn't have a clue where I was although outside looked familiar. I came out of my room and saw that I was in the local hospital where I had stayed several times before. I now felt much safer and thought it was Friday but it was Saturday so obviously I had lost a day of my life, totally wiped out by the drugs. My mind needed to rest and boy did it, apparently they had transported me here during Friday when I was comatosed, I don't recall any of it or the whole day, scary thought but it needed to happen as I was manic and out of my mind.

I struck up conversations with other patients, which made me feel a little easier but I still had the paranoia as though somebody was still trying to get me. Darell came to visit me every day whilst I was in there and yet again I started smoking! The hospital had changed in the last 4 years, it seemed like chaos, the majority of staff didn't have time to talk to patients and there was far too much paperwork. By the way if any politician gets to read this, MORE money needs to be invested in Mental Health!

I found it very difficult to sleep in hospital, as I felt awfully paranoid. I remember one night I woke up and heard a helicopter overhead, I thought *'that is it they are here and are going to get me.'* I rang Darell in the middle of the night and screamed down the phone to come and get me. Then I imagined heads floating around the hospital ward like something out of Harry Potter. I was frightened for my life and the staff had to calm me down. I think I took a sleeping tablet to calm me down, I don't remember exactly.

Gradually I began to improve and chat to the other patients more and they all had their different stories and I was trying to help them and also help myself at the same time. I was still scared so I asked for Level 3 supervision from staff, this means that someone is with you 24/7 even when you go to the toilet. It's strange at first but I got used to it and this really helped me as I was able to talk to staff about my problems and slowly my paranoia and anxiety attacks receded and the demons were slowly leaving me. I felt like I was returning back to myself, and being able to rationalize my mind. So it just shows you, that if staff had time to invest in the patients how much quicker your recovery is. Whilst I was in hospital, my psychiatrist referred to me to a Chaplin who was Catholic, she understood everything I was saying about the mind being able to absorb external factors, hence the fact they perform exorcisms which are not normally spoken about.

One night during my stay, there was a great deal of commotion going on and this guy came in and started to throw chairs and aggressively bang his head on the glass window. This set me off again and I was scared, so I requested to have some overnight leave as I wasn't going to sleep knowing that he was on the ward. After a Ward Review with my psychiatrist, I was able to take some overnight leave.

I still felt a little scared at home and on that night I started to have a panic attack because I felt evil energies again, Darell my partner rang up the hospital and I requested to speak to one of the nurses that I trusted and he understood my spiritual nature. He calmed me down just by talking to him and I felt so much better.

I had increased leave for a week and slowly continued to get better. My employer was fantastic and supported me 100% especially my boss Glynis. She even came to visit me a few times in hospital and came to a review with my psychiatrist which was very helpful. I think she was quite shocked at some of the patients who had self-harmed as this can be very distressing.

I am not sure why this episode came out of the blue, the only thing I can think of is I had a lot of stress at the time along with heightened spiritual activity, which lead me towards another episode.

I had about a month off work and then came back on a staggered basis, which was great and worked well with my mindset. I also saw an Occupational Health advisor who supported me through my return to work. My work colleagues were also supportive and so understanding. I quickly got back into the swing of things and work returned to normal, although my work-load was reduced which was beneficial.

A few months later Darell and I decided to go to Rhodes with some friends to relax. We had such a laugh and really enjoyed ourselves, it was a refreshing tonic after another episode. Each time, it was hard for even me to comprehend what happens each time.

My talks were going really well and I also attended workshops to help myself and went to see a spiritual teacher, who really helped me. I attended one of her circles, however I think I scared one of the other ladies. The teacher taught me how to protect myself against unknown energies and also remain grounded. She also told me some things that I knew were true and confirmed everything that I thought, was indeed correct. If you are open and have a sensitive mind, it is amazing what our world offers. There are signs from spirit/past loved ones everywhere, you just need to focus your mind rather than constantly over thinking and analysing the arse out of every situation. I have to remain careful and in check as if I get carried away I end up going into an episode. There is an extremely fine line between spirituality and Mental Health. A mental hospital is one of the most spiritual places I have ever been to, apart from a church and the majority of in-patients have had a spiritual/energy experience and openly talk about it on the wards. Darell was a little concerned about this excessive spiritual activity each time, so advised me to perhaps stay away from circles and just concentrate on getting myself fully well.

The house was looking great and Darell had totally renovated the whole of the garden. He had done the ground-works for the new conservatory, which looked amazing, and we had a new kitchen installed by one of his mates, which is a bonus for being in the construction trade. Darell wanted to get another dog so we ended up with a brown and white puppy springer spaniel who apparently was the well behaved one of the litter. This was definitely not the case and the little thing was hyper from day one! Totally different from Boris. We named him Charlie! I will leave you to guess why!

9
If You Can Visualise

During our stay at Witham, I spent a lot of time going to see my Granny Toby as Grandad had died a while back and she was on her own. She was in a warden assisted place in Maldon and she loved it. She was out nearly every night playing bingo, chess, and quizzes. You name it she was there. I remember I bought an Audi TT, which I absolutely loved and only had for a year; I took Gran out in it one day, and seeing her try to get out of a low car was hilarious. We did have a laugh though. She was my mum's mum and I could definitely see traits in my mum of gran! She died at the age of 94, of old age, which was extremely sad but the best way to go. My sister did an amazing speech at her funeral that had everyone in tears. I still miss all my grandparents today but know they are around as I sense them. It might be that I hear a song that reminds me of them or smell a certain fragrance. I believe 100% in afterlife, there are too many coincidences and things that happen to make it not be true. I just wish people were more open to it but perhaps that will happen in later years.

The following year I had another mini episode, but luckily Darell took me out of work before anything happened. I had a really weird experience though just before Darell took me out; I was talking to one of my work colleagues about her dad who had passed away earlier in the year and it felt like some-one moved into my body. It reminded me of the film *'Ghost'* where Patrick Swayze moves into Whoopi Goldberg's body. The next day I went into episode, I started to have rushing thoughts and started to get high again and became full of extreme positivity. My intentions in this mode are the best, as I want to help everyone become a better person; the trouble is, it's to my own detriment. I self-medicated with Darrell's help and took some time off work. The spirits/energies were back, what did they want from me? I remembered all that the spiritual teacher had said and remained grounded and calm.

I spent a month off work to recuperate and get myself back to some kind of normal so I could concentrate. During this particular episode I remember thinking I wanted to move, so I asked the universe to provide me with a house with 3 bedrooms, wood stove, butler sink, open wooded beams and a large garden. We had out grown the house, although Darell had done loads of work to it, which had put the value up a great deal. I started to look on right move and found this house in Coggeshall and it had everything I had requested. I went to look at it on my own initially and was the last person on that day to view it. I fell in love straight away so just had to convince Darell now that it was a great idea. He was a bit dubious as it was on a busy road but I managed to persuade him. We sold our house in a day and moved within two months. This particular house was also on my vision board so the universe had worked its magic - I was so happy! It's actually amazing how much crap you collate over the years and we soon managed to fill up the new place. Darell decorated the whole house in our taste of colour and started to work on the garden - that guy never stops!

After settling in, we hired a camper van for a week during the summer holidays and went down to the New Forest with the dogs, it was brilliant and I loved the freedom of the camper van. So me being me, decided to buy a caravan when I got back home. I thought to myself we could have lovely holidays in the UK with the dogs enjoying the English Countryside.

I started to get even more involved in completing talks at schools and setting up mindfulness and meditation sessions to help not just me, but also help other people. The mind is so powerful and you CAN achieve anything if you set your mind to it. I was also looking for three things to put on my Gran's grave who had died 4 years previously. I wanted a ribbon, a silver cross and an artificial flower.

Glynis (my boss at the time) sent me some lovely flowers, which had a beautiful ribbon on, so I used this as one of the items. Darell then bought me an artificial flower from the local nursery, so it was just the silver cross that I was after.

The next day I took the dogs for a walk in the park and I was drawn to this old lady that was sitting on one of the park benches. We started chatting about random things and all of a sudden she said I have something for you. Now bearing in mind I had never met this person before - she got out her purse and handed me a silver cross, my chin hit the floor! I couldn't believe it as this is what I had been looking for. I thanked her and explained the reason I wanted this and she said she knew and that was why she gave it to me! Well how random and spooky is that. I think that is when the realisation finally hit me with such certainty that there is something definitely more to the world than meets the eye. I have been through a tremendous amount but this seriously was spooky!

There were several other things that happened to me over the next month that were unexplainable but fascinating, however that is a different story. I have always been interested in the spirit world and have believed in angels ever since I read the book *'Angels in my hair'* by Lorna Byrne. She is an amazing woman and I have attended lots of her talks/events, even Darell came to one! I practice with Angel cards and started to do readings, one Christmas I did an event fair at Coggeshall Village hall. I only charged £10 donation just to cover my costs and saw 10 people. They all were extremely impressed with my readings and said that I should be charging more. I just enjoy it and am not interested in earning a living out of it.

Things were going well, I loved spending time with my family and often saw my nieces, mum and sister. We went to Centre Parcs again one year, and had a fab time down the rapids even if we did end up all battered and bruised. Actually I think that is all we did - swim, eat and talk! We also had a few wider family events, which were great as I get on really well with all the extended family.

One of Darrell's close friends had a baby boy called Jack, so Darell became a godfather; he was over the moon as we chose early on not to have kids. I think one of the reasons was because I didn't want our children being affected or having a Mental Health condition like me as they say it can be hereditary. Also I would have had to come off my medication whilst pregnant and the risk was too high. I just spent time and spoilt my nieces who bring me great pleasure and Darell sees Jack when he can. Work was going well and I used to go up to London once a month, however it came as a bit of a blow one day when my manager advised me that my job would be moving to London and there was no role in Witham. I was gutted as I didn't want to move to London, I had moved out to the country so the travel to London wasn't particularly easy and also it would be extra cost. I decided not to go and I was made redundant after 6 years. Rather than let it affect me, I saw it as an opportunity and I walked into another job within about a week, Hurrah! It was an insurance company based in Chelmsford. The boss was great and we got on really well. I think I shocked him in the interview as his office was huge and I said when I walked in there *'Wow this office is huge, all it needs now is a bed!'* What possessed me to say that I don't know, but he found it really funny and hired me on the spot. I met his wife and sister too who were also extremely lovely, so things were looking up. The office atmosphere was great and everyone seemed really happy, I got involved in loads of interesting things and the other Personal Assistant there was great. She really helped me and supported me in showing me the ropes. It was extremely busy but I loved it.

One of my close friends at the time, Nicola, was having problems with her boyfriend and one night I had a very distressing phone call from her saying that he had hit her. She was so frightened bless her and was with her neighbour waiting for the police. I made the decision to drop everything and go and be with her to see if I could help. The police arrested him and we went back into the house. I stayed with Nicola that night as she didn't want to be alone. Trouble is I didn't get much sleep as I was paranoid that the boyfriend would come back and attack us, or something. I think I had about 2 hours sleep, which is not good for my mental health. I went to work the next day, which was extremely busy then spent another night at Nicola's to keep her company. Again we didn't have a good night so I remember Darell popping round that morning as he was worried about me and suggested that Nicola and her little boy Lewis stay at ours which she agreed to. At least then I would be able to get a good night's sleep. I felt like a zombie when I went into work as I had serious sleep deprivation. I was extremely emotionally and broke down in front of the Human Resources lady and told her about the situation and also that I had Bipolar. She couldn't believe it and said that she would support me through this. The state I was in I should have gone home but I was in a new job and I didn't want to lose it, so I stupidly went back to work. BIG MISTAKE! My mind was doing somersaults and I could feel the energies around me again as if something bad was about to happen, I am still now mortified as to what happened next.

10
Paranoia Overload

Back in the office they were talking about horror films which didn't help me with how vulnerable I felt and this brought back all my worst nightmares from the film I watched when I was 13 - Nightmare on Elm Street. It still sends chills down my spine now; it was the most horrific film, and as I said before, I have spent the majority of my life suffering uncontrollable nightmares because of it. My imagination is extremely vivid anyhow and my mind started racing even more. The next thing I knew I had grabbed one of the girls and sat her down in the kitchen and explained to her that the world was about to end but it would be okay as I would win the lottery soon. Why would I say this? I had lost my mind again and suddenly felt the evil energy all around me. I jumped up and shouted *'Quick now we must go!'* And ran out into the main office. There were about 10 people in the office all busily concentrating on their work and I bombarded into the room and I screamed out *'All of you just shut the fuck up and listen to what I am about to say as it is extremely important!' 'Don't you realise how lucky you are and how grateful you should be?'* I was then flipping between negative and positive, pointing fingers at people and saying that aliens were attacking the planet. I then shouted at this poor guy and said I fell in love with him the first time I saw him and what would he say if I asked him to marry me! Poor bloke looked completely dumbfounded, I still remember his face now, and his shocked and terrified expression. He didn't say anything and I didn't even wait for the response as I had now spun into paranoid mode and thought my worst nightmare was in the room. Negativity was everywhere and I slammed my body against the wall as if I was being attacked by an invisible force of repulsion. I was terror-stricken, unable to speak and grasped this girl's hair to pull her out the way and then bolted out of the room and down the stairs screaming at people to run. This guy was in front of me and also started to run as I had sent him into a total panic and he didn't even know why. I suppose your natural instinct kicks in and if someone is screaming behind you, automatically you run, no questions asked. I proceeded to lock the door but had no key so was acting out the motion, it was just in my imagination.

I frantically starting looking for my dream car outside the building which is an Audi R8, but couldn't see it, so then was desperately searching for some kind of recognisable landmark or something that looked familiar to help me. I kept running round the car park and then stopped briefly at this group of people to demonstrate my karate skills which I have never even attempted to do in my life. I turned round and a woman approached me, appearing in my mind, very angry and like a bully from my school days. She had a menacing look, so I screamed and ran off in more of a panic. What was I thinking? The trouble was, I wasn't thinking, I had lost the plot again, it felt like non-existent beings were forcing me to do things I didn't want to do. I felt like my head was going to explode and the thoughts were stifling. People from the office were collating in the car park and trying to get me to calm down but I didn't trust anyone and I was firing out accusations left, right, and centre. I don't think they knew what on earth was going on and it was definitely not something they had ever witnessed before.

Suddenly the police arrived and detained me and put me in the back of the police car. The young policeman was brilliant and he managed to calm me down within a few minutes and BANG the realisation suddenly hit me. What on earth had I done and why? I could see one of the girls crying from the window of the police car and she was so upset, I felt mortified and helpless. I was overcome with feelings of wanting to get out of the car to say sorry, but it was too late, the damage had been done and we drove off. There was no turning back the clock and how would I explain to her what had happened? I didn't understand it myself. The second police officer came to see me about 15 minutes later and I was taken to A&E in the company of the police officer who was so professional and spoke to me like a proper human being. By this time I had calmed down quite considerably so was able to have a normal decent conversation. It wasn't long before I was taken into a room to be assessed by a nurse, they have to get two people to sit in the interview as they don't know the mental state of the patient and they need to protect themselves. I was asked loads of questions then left alone with my own thoughts. I kept going over and over in my mind why had this happened again? Why oh why?

Darell arrived about an hour later and I have never felt so happy to see him, we hugged tightly and I didn't want to let him go, I was so embarrassed about what I had done and didn't know quite how to tell him. We sat and chatted for a couple of hours whilst the nurses decided my fate, all I knew was, the last place I wanted to go to was the local mental hospital. I hated that place and it gave me serious nightmares, I had spent too many times there and I was petrified of the whole environment and what it stood for. Darell cheered me up no end and I was so thankful to have him in my life. For what seemed like an eternity and no-one entering the room; without warning, it seemed like the whole world descended on us, we had a social worker, two psychiatrists, one mental health nurse and a trainee nurse. Cosy I thought and here we go again. The social worker started to pipe on about how many qualifications he had and a master's degree in some subject I had never heard of. I switched off straight away and thought why did he have the need to justify himself to me? He continued to convey his words and when addressing me spoke to me like I was 5 years old. This sent me from 0 to 100 in a millisecond, and I screamed *'Don't speak to me like I an idiot, I know more about my mental health condition than you will ever know.'* He suddenly flinched and his face switched, I knew he was not impressed at all. I then dismissed him like a ton of bricks and directed my attention to the other Doctor who was sitting there with his mouth open. When he spoke he was extremely nervous and initially started stuttering. The thing is though, when you are in a manic state your senses are heightened and for some reason you get superman hearing, it's all very bizarre. The social worker stupidly muttered something under his breath and I heard it! Big mistake! So as quick as a flash I spun round and said *'What the fuck did you say?'* He looked stunned and then denied it and said *'Nothing.'* This is the worst thing you could ever do as I absolutely loathe people who lie anyhow, let alone when I am in an episode.

I didn't stop there and I carried on and said *'I suggest you tell me what you said as I heard you mutter under your breath'.* And do you know what, he then admitted he did say something, he said that I was rude! Well there you go, why lie? I said thank you and that was all I asked. I think our relationship after that incident was doomed and I could sense he didn't like me at all. This was the final straw and now he had no time for me. The meeting went on for ages and they came to the conclusion that I was to go to the hospital. I went to get a quick drink with Darell and ended up losing the plot again with the nurse in charge as her breath smelt of smoke. I personally didn't think this was the environment to be smelling of smoke, she wasn't happy at all and I must admit I didn't go about it in the best of manners. From memory, I totally shouted her down in front of all her work colleagues. I had embarrassed her and now she didn't like me. I was building up enemies all over A&E, not great considering they had the ultimate say in my destiny.

After lengthy consultations I finally agreed to go to hospital and when I was walking down the corridor with the social worker and Darell everything seemed fine. Then BANG, all of a sudden, paranoia hit me like a thunderbolt, as they opened the doors into the main reception to A&E. I started to get nervy again and automatically I grabbed onto the railing and sat on the floor and screamed *'I don't want to go to that fucking dreadful place!'* I pleaded to Darell to do anything to stop this, in my mind I thought they were taking me away to murder me, I was convinced and was in a state of panic. I was screaming *'HELP me HELP me,'* as I frantically tried to remain glued to the pole. Darell seemed not to hear me and neither did the social worker it was like they had turned into robots. They pulled me up by the legs with two other guys supporting my arms and started to carry me out, I was screaming to anybody and everybody that could hear me. Do you know what, no-one who sat in A&E turned round, it was as if time had stopped still and they had all been brain washed. I couldn't believe what was happening. It felt like I was in some sort of horror film.

I had a major panic attack outside as I thought this is it, they are going to kill me, they were whispering and I couldn't hear what they were saying so this made it worse. I was so convinced that I screamed out as loud as I could *'God, Jesus, please, please, help me!'* All of a sudden Darell and the social worker dropped my legs and I was being sucked back into the A&E through the doors and back to the room. I was hyper ventilating by this time and the staff were trying to get me to breathe and calm down. I have never, ever, been so petrified in my life and it took me a while to settle down. All I kept saying to the staff was thank you, thank you, thank you, you have saved my life, as genuinely in my mind I thought they had. I was so relieved.

When I eventually recovered after taking some water, I had two security guards sitting either side of me. It all felt a bit strange and then Darell was allowed back in the room and they abruptly left. I was still a bit wary of him and wondered why he had done what had he had done. We started to have an argument and he really pushed me to breaking point so I punched him right in the mouth, BOOM! What was wrong with me? I was never violent but I had this hidden aggression that sparked from no-where. He grabbed his mouth and then the door flew open and the security guards pulled Darell out of the room. I saw Darell look at me with sheer horror on his face, holding his cut lip, which was pouring with blood. I was shouting *'I am so sorry honey'* but he wasn't listening and the staff took him away. So I was left alone again which seemed like forever, lost in my own thoughts of sheer panic and confused delusion. It felt like I wasn't in control of my own body and someone was making me do these horrible things. I felt helpless and wanted to cry but felt numb inside and had no tears to shed. The two security guards then re-entered the room and resumed their position either side of me. I did feel safe and protected and it also helped that one of them was extremely good looking, but knew it, so I thought it would be a challenge to bring him down a peg or two. So, I proceeded for the next two hours or so to have banter and make the other guard laugh out loud.

It was a surreal situation as I became the performer making everybody laugh, it was all very bizarre and staff just kept coming in and out of the room. After what seemed like ages, the social worker who didn't like me, came back in the room and said that they would have to **forcibly** take me to hospital if I was not to come quietly. In fact his words were, *'we will strap you to a bed and wheel you out in front of everyone, and do you want that?'* Charming - is that how you treat patients? I was adamant that I was not going anywhere so eventually they ended up restraining me and injecting me with many drugs, in order for me to get some rest and much needed sleep.

11
The Zoo

I woke the following morning in the same room, feeling all disorientated and wondered what had just happened. I had blacked out which was probably all of the drugs. A lovely ambulance woman then came in and kindly spoke to me, I instantly warmed to her and let my guard down. She said that they were going to take me to a safe place and everything would be OK. Of course I trusted her, so I went in the ambulance, which was only a short ride. At the other end I walked through some corridors and was led into a room that had 4 walls, a window, a crash mat in the corner, two chairs, a separate shower cubicle and a toilet. What on earth was this and where was I? The door slammed shut and that was it. I was left alone yet again in this cold room that had cameras in the corner and an eerie spooky feeling inside.

The feelings of someone invisible being around me had calmed down a bit by then, but inside I was silently panicking. What fate was waiting for me? The door then opened and a staff member who I recognised from my previous admission to hospital came inside. I was overjoyed to see him and he asked what I would like to eat and that my wish was his command. I felt elated and I managed to contain the urge to go over and hug him. You don't realise that when you are wrenched away from your family and left in isolation, you welcome any friendly face, believe me. He brought me a lovely meal and I was so hungry and devoured it within a second and I even got some dessert. It was very short lived, as he then disappeared. A different member of staff that had closed the door behind him was now sitting by the window on the laptop and making notes on my actions. Being alone with yourself and just four walls, you have nothing to do apart from pace around the room dealing with your own thoughts. I noticed that the staff changed every hour, made some notes, did a quick handover and then were off duty.

Sometimes the door was left open and I was allowed a chair near the door, so I could speak to the staff but it all went pear shaped when one of the staff members, a young boy, was being ultra-cocky and it started to wind me up. I had spent about 45 minutes chatting to him and I suppose building trust with him, then I flipped again and tried to test him. The dark menacing energies consumed me. I kept telling him to pull the panic button as I was about to throw the chairs across the room. When he didn't, I chucked the chairs from one side of the room to the next. He didn't seem phased about this so I continued and said that I would punch him on the nose if he didn't pull the panic button. He responded by saying "*you wouldn't do that, as I know you and trust you.*" For some reason this outraged me further, so instead of punching him on the nose, I punched him in the kidneys and BANG that was it! The alarm was sounded and I was thrust back into the isolated room. Now the question is, why did I do that? Why did I penalise what I had built up and now I was back to square one, locked up in the room with staff just staring at me through the little window? I was a fool and was definitely not in my right mind. I began to think I was an animal, a tiger of all things, and I paced round the inside of my cage and even began to roar like one, the staff must have thought I was crazy, but do you know the reason I did it? I was trying to remain in control and sane. I could feel myself losing it and then I started to jump up and down on the crash mat like an ape banging my chest and doing all of the ape noises. I now know what animals feel like being locked up in a zoo and everyone staring at them. Believe me, it is horrendous and you feel totally trapped; poor animals, and more to the point, poor me.

Game 2, next instalment - I was so bored and extremely agitated so I thought it would be funny to play a trick on another staff member and was trying to occupy myself and remain level headed. I pretended I was locked in the bathroom and was signalling to the lady at the window and mouthing that I couldn't get out. She came in and when she approached me, I jumped out and blocked the exit door so she couldn't get back out. I was goading her to press the alarm and prancing about. She immediately pressed the alarm, which was totally right, and the troops arrived and the door closed again. They both looked at me like I was a pile of shit on their shoe and after making some sarcastic remarks, she was left alone and then preceded to blank me for the rest of her duration. Her behaviour made me worse and I was getting so distressed but she didn't care, I had obviously humiliated and annoyed her, so now she was going to repay me by totally ignoring me. I banged on the window, called her all the names under the sun and my mouth was so very dry. She refused to give me any water. Is this really how a patient should be treated? I was appalled and shocked and even more so when she proceeded to lie about me in handover to the next person, who I actually had created a bond with. The replacement nurse looked astonished and this other woman had clearly made stuff up. I noticed on the notes that she had written some bullshit down which never happened, but hey I'm the mad one right so who was going to believe me? I felt totally betrayed and mortified. Questioning why I was doing what I was doing and also why was I still locked in this room?

As the day/night went on I became increasingly agitated and felt like I would be locked in there forever. There was no escape and I felt like the walls were drawing into me, time stood still in there and I felt claustrophobic and nauseous. It was the worse experience I had ever encountered, to the point that I banged on the window to let me out and pleaded with them, I kept repeating over and over again *'HELP me, HELP me, HELP me, PLEASE someone!'* The next thing I knew, Darell had walked in, saw me like this, and he lost his marbles. He behaved like me earlier, blew his top and yelled at the staff to open the door and let me out. His words were extremely explicit and when he ran in I just crumbled to the floor. All my energy and strength had disappeared from my body and I wailed *'I can't do this anymore,*

I want it to end.' I wanted to die and Darell knew it. He cuddled me so tightly and cried too and he said *"you CAN do this, you are a strong person."* All I kept saying was *"No this is it for me, I can't, it's too much."* It was hellish, I NEVER went into hospital feeling suicidal, but became suicidal in that room. How anyone can cope being locked up in solitary confinement for a period of time when they are sane, let alone if someone is experiencing bouts of psychosis is beyond me.

Darell comforted me for ages until I managed to control my sobbing. He was adamant that he would get me out ASAP; I felt hopeful and knew that he would keep to his word. He spoke sternly to the staff and demanded for me to be let out into the fresh air. I didn't even realise that there was an outside space next to the room where you could have some fresh air. No-one had told me about this. It was only 12 foot square and had high brick walls so there was no chance of escape even if you wanted to. I was extremely grateful for the fresh air, it was lovely and the sun was on my face, which I hadn't seen for 2 days. Darell said that they had offered a bed for me that was a 4 hour drive away and he refused, as I would have been even more isolated away from home and family and friends. This was the reason why I was still locked in this room, as there were no local beds available anywhere. On a side point this is a real worry for any future incidents and the lack of availability. Darell left promising me that he would sort something out. Again I was left alone and noticed a group of staff waiting outside the room. I thought this can only mean one thing and knew that I was going to be restrained again and injected. It's happened to me too many times before to not know what they were planning, so I laid face down on the crash mat waiting for what I knew what going to happen. Bingo - I even heard them say *'oh look she has got herself into position.'* I was dragged from the crash mat and held on the cold floor and injected, and yes I did feel like an animal. After they had finished I lay on the floor for a bit and just pondered what to do next. It's amazing what thoughts go through your mind when you are in captivity.

All of a sudden I sprung up and started to dance around the place singing, but do you know what, I didn't care. I lost all my inhibitions and was showing my boobs to the staff. It was as if I had a self-destruct button that had been pushed on and off for the last 2 days. Eventually the drugs hit and I blacked out again. The next day I was allowed to go onto the main ward and mix with the other patients, so at least I had some human contact, although saying that, it was like World War 3. Patients were screaming at each other and running about, it was mayhem. I thought *'what the hell'* and joined in. Darell came in to visit and was trying to arrange for the doctor to meet me. I had calmed down a lot being away from the awful Section 136 room, which was giving me nightmares. I spent the whole day wandering around aimlessly and wanted and craved contact with my friends and family. When you are in hospital you feel like no-one cares and you feel abandoned, even though you are not. My friend Nicola came to visit me, which was great and cheered me up for a small amount of time.

When bedtime was looming I was told that I would have to go back into the dreaded Section 136 room, I was petrified and then out of no-where this lovely girl kindly volunteered to take my place for the night as she knew and could feel how scared I was. Unfortunately the staff would not allow this so I was escorted back to the living nightmare where I spent the night in fear. I was allowed out again the following day, hurrah! Freedom and was back on the ward. Darell had arranged for the doctor to see me and I was actually beginning to feel a bit back to my old self; I felt a sense of hope. Darell was brilliant and so supportive. He agreed to look after me and said that being in hospital was making me worse and no good for my recovery. Darell managed to get me out from what felt like prison and I was so relieved I wanted to bellow from the rooftops and celebrate. The feeling is incredible to know that you have been released from a secure unit and can now do things that a lot of people take for granted. I certainly don't and have never done since I was first sectioned in 2003. I was trying to think back what had triggered this major relapse and episode of mania. It must have been a combination of the stressful job, high-energy spiritual encounters and extremely positive events that all happened within one month. My brain can't cope with all of this heightened activity and I have to ensure that I remain grounded and avoid any stressful situations. The company I'd been at dismissed me, which was a shame as I was really enjoying the work and liked the people there. I suppose once again it is a lack of education and perhaps if I'd had the opportunity to explain they might have understood but we will never know.

12

New Beginnings

I spent the next 6 weeks relaxing, meditating and going for walks to try and grasp a better understanding as to why this kept happening to me, and what I needed to do to try and prevent the episodes. They seemed to be getting worse and I had literally no control. I had no job and didn't know where I was going to find one either. Glynis was concerned about me and had been ringing me up to find out how I was. I didn't want to talk to anyone and felt so embarrassed about what had happened so I turned into a bit of a hermit for 6 weeks. Darell was so supportive but even this episode took it out of him, he struggled big time with this one, and we nearly split up. Glynis didn't give up though and she spoke to Roy the director at the insurance company I used to work for and managed to set up an interview for me. I was so grateful for that so brushed up on my interview techniques and prepared for the day. On the day of the interview I was shitting a brick, I did know Roy from before but only slightly. I thought to myself if I am going to succeed in this meeting I need to be myself 100%, no barriers, no masks. Roy was either going to like me or find me totally annoying and as for my diagnosis well if you are not honest how are you ever going to change this world and reduce stigma and discrimination. Roy told me that a large amount of people had applied for the job and he had recently seen a Personal Assistant who had looked after a Lord. I thought blimey, I definitely have some competition here. He said *'so Liz how are you going to impress me?'* I thought here goes, I am going to be totally honest, as I made the grand mistake last time in not being honest, and look where it got me.

I told Roy I was diagnosed with Bipolar back in 2003 and basically a quick story of all that I had been through. When I finally managed to lift his chin from the floor, Roy couldn't believe it and said that I was the last person in the world he thought would have Bipolar as I always seemed so happy and positive. He continued to say that it didn't matter and how brave I was and that he would support me 100% and also when could I start? I nearly fainted, I couldn't believe my ears, and went all nervous and clumsy. I was so gob smacked and was over the moon that he had offered me a job, I actually gave him a high five! What was I thinking - but hey why change my personality. The reason I was so taken aback, was because the majority of my employers haven't adopted the same attitude or approach and it just shows you how mental health can be a barrier for many in the workplace.

Darell was extremely pleased too and gave me a huge hug and so were all my family. I started in June 2018 and was an Executive Assistant to Roy and the Senior Leadership Team. I knuckled down and started to make the job my own. Roy is so laid back and such a great boss, as long as I told him what I was doing and where I was going, he was happy. I started to really enjoy it and things were going great at home too, Darell was sorting out the house and we spent lots of time with the family. I loved my nieces coming over to visit and we used to spend lots of time going to the cinema and for days out with my sister and Mum too. I had given up drinking 2 years previously and felt so much better. I was doing everything that the doctor ordered and more and was feeling good. We recently had a log cabin delivered which Darell was currently doing up. Unfortunately we couldn't get planning permission on the bit of land we had so we decided to go for the log cabin option and make it an extended garden. In November we had booked a Caribbean Cruise so I got super excited about this, it seemed that everything was going great, my job, our house, the holiday, perfect. The cruise was just how I imagined it and we had the best time ever, Darell morphed into a positive person, which was great as I can't stand negativity, it sucks the life out of me. I call people like that dementors out of Harry Potter as you can literally feel the life being sucked out. It's either that or mood hoovers. I know we all have challenges in life, which can be extremely difficult, but it is how you face them. Now I am not saying that people who have depression can just snap out of it believe me I tried, but I am talking about the day to day things that people say about the weather, work and life. It's all about your mindset and how you choose to be. The weather was amazing and so were all the different islands.

I got back and was very elated from the holiday, and my sleep had been a bit all over the place. There seemed to be a lot of negativity at work and I was beginning to get a tad pissed off with it. To the point I nearly lost it in one of the meetings. I think I knew that I wasn't quite right as I took myself off home one day and that weekend it all kicked off again - I was agitated, short tempered, and my moods were high. Darell and I were walking round the park with the dogs when I flipped and for some reason thought I was on a film set of the recent film, *'Quiet in the Woods,'* where people have to walk round in silence to avoid being eaten by monsters. I became convinced that Darell was about to kill me so I grabbed Marion from work, who luckily for me happened to be in the park walking her dog at the same time and started whispering in her ear and telling her to be quiet or they will hear us. Marion was brilliant and took it all in her stride and she went along with what I was saying and was talking to me calmly. I don't think she quite understood what was going on and I don't think she knew how much she helped me. Darell had called an ambulance as he could see I had flipped which made me worse as I knew where that was taking me.

I started to go into a panic attack so he agreed to cancel it and I went for a little walk with Marion whilst she reassured me. I can't thank Marion enough for what she did for me that day. I thought Darell was the enemy again and was after me so I refused to get into his car, the neighbours had to come and pick me up and I stayed round there for about 2 hours to calm down. I started to return to normal or what I thought was normal and went back home with Darell. For some reason I started to antagonise Darell and wind him up, he obviously started to get annoyed but I didn't stop, it was like I was goading him to get his anger out. He did explode and then I went into a rage. I started to flip out and was pretending that I was on a murder scene in film mode; I always seem to go into this state when this happens. I kept flipping into different films, thinking I had seen Robbie Williams in the garden, from barking like a dog from the film Hangover and then dancing provocatively. The weird thing is I can remember all what I was doing and can still now but I couldn't stop myself. The only way I can describe it, is it felt like I was a puppet and someone was making me doing these things and I had no control. It was frightening but I thought it was normal. Darell was extremely worried and couldn't control me so rang the doctors who came straight out to the house to assess me. Trouble is, this provoked me as they went over the same thing again. I was getting worse and even threatened one of the doctors verbally. This sent alarm bells to them and they called the police along with two ambulance crew members. I was petrified when the police arrived, as all I was thinking in my mind was that they were going to take me away and kill me. I was completely convinced that this was going to happen. The lady police officer talked to me calmly and advised that I would be going with them to the hospital. They walked me out and Darell looked mortified; he was desperately trying to avoid this at all costs as he knew how much I hated the hospital but unfortunately it had gone too far again and I was now a danger to myself.

When I got to the ambulance I panicked and wouldn't move. The officers didn't know what was going on in my head and there was no way in a million years I was going to tell them what I thought. They were trying to think of ways to get me inside the car and then all of a sudden the lady police officer did something completely out of the box, talk about quick thinking. She said to me *'will you trust me and go in the van if I do 5 star jumps?'* I know weird hey but it worked as she had my attention, I trusted her and to her credit, she did it and I went into the back of the van. They whisked me away to the hospital in Colchester to be assessed and I flipped again in the unit so they put me in a room on my own again to calm down. As you know this makes me more agitated so I just paced round the room like an animal again. Eventually they moved me to the local hospital so I spent the night there. I didn't sleep a wink as I was petrified that the staff would kill me. My thoughts were doing overtime in my head again.

Darell bought me in a bag of clothes the next day along with my angels and comfort things. I begged him to try and get me out as I was convinced that something bad was going to happen. That night I laid awake in my bed with the light on ALL night, having cold sweats. My mind was working overtime. I know sleep is crucial to my well-being, but I was utterly paranoid and scared beyond my wits. When Darell came in the morning, I was in a terrible state and was crying and pleading with him to get me out. Remarkably he agreed as he could see that it was mentally and physically making me worse remaining in hospital. So he demanded to see the doctors who happened to be located on the ward that day; an answer to my prayers. I left all the talking to Darell and about an hour later I was out; freedom again and fresh air. Until you have experienced this kind of trauma, we all can take this for granted. So please, for one moment, just STOP what you are doing and appreciate and feel grateful for the fact you are alive in the fresh air and not confined to a secure hospital. Be grateful for what you have and enjoy every moment of your life.

I was off work for about 3 weeks and Roy and the Senior Leadership were extremely supportive. Roy and Gabby came and visited me at home to see if I was OK which was really nice and made me feel supported. I went to see an Occupational Health advisor who was great, he assessed my ability to return to work on a phased basis initially and then full time after that. Glynis also got involved and advised Roy what could have happened to bring on this relapse and also to look out for signs in the future.

So here I was again on the road to recovery, I threw myself into self -help exercises again, mindfulness, meditation and well-being to help my mental health, and then by Christmas I was virtually back to my old self. Roy and Gabby conducted a review with me to check my workload and suggested delegating some work and also advising me not to take too much on. I became the co-chair champion for Mental Health for Diversity & Inclusion at work along with a lovely girl called Valerie who was also extremely passionate about Mental Health. Just before Christmas, my good friend Ashley and I were talking about mental health in the workplace and she currently works for the NHS. We were talking about instructors training staff up to become Mental Health First Aiders. This got my mind thinking so I put a proposal together to Roy with a view to me becoming an in-house instructor, saving money for the company by getting people trained up and also doing something that I am so passionate about. I was over the moon when Roy agreed so I attended the course in February 2019 and have since delivered a couple of two day courses and trained 22 Mental Health First Aiders in the workplace. This is a massive step forward in today's society and I can only hope that the government pass a law so it becomes mandatory. Mental health is just as important as physical health so we should address this too.

In March 2019 I was selected as one of the finalists for the Women's Daily Mail Inspirational awards, I was gob smacked and attended an awards ceremony along with my close friends, Mum and Darell in London. It was an incredible evening, I didn't win, however I was so pleased that I had been recognised for all the voluntary and charity work I do supporting people with mental health issues. I arranged two charity events recently raising money for Young Minds and Mind to the value of £2k and my friends and family were all so supportive and also received an award from Lloyds for all the voluntary work I have done. I received £4k for Young Minds and then my company matched in with another £4k, which was amazing. I was over the moon and so was the charity. I am always doing events at work to raise the profile of mental health and raise money for like-minded charities.

The more I speak out about mental health it seems the more opportunities keep arising which I love as I really want to break down the stigma and educate people. I now also do Positive Mindset workshops along with my friend Angela. We cover visualisation, the law of attraction, mindfulness, meditation, salt lamps, essential oils, angel card readings. We have conducted two so far and they have been really successful - we are planning more in the future too. I would love to arrange a mini festival with local bands which will be my next project, so watch this space! I also provide Angelic Reiki Healing and angel card readings in my log cabin which I absolutely love. I keep myself grounded and relaxed and I enjoy helping people, which is what it is all about.

2019 has been a big change and shift in my life and I seem to be much more in control of my mental health and well-being. I recently went to a Buddha healing/meditation in a log cabin in Writtle. My close friend Nicola encouraged me to go so I thought I would try it. I do love my Buddha's, I think I have about 10 all over the house and I'm planning to get a big one in the garden. The master Buddha was over from the US, so it was all very exciting. Nicola was beside her self and kept saying I knew you were to come here today for a reason. Nicola is so funny and we have known each other for years, she thinks like me about the laws of attraction and the universe so we are on the same wave length. Before the master Buddha started at the event he just asked the group whether anyone wanted any healing or had any requests. Now I wouldn't normally do this as it was with a group of people I didn't know but I put my hand up and said jokingly *'you can cure my Bipolar.'* He acknowledged it and nodded calmly.

During the meditation the weirdest thing happened to me and I will explain so you can try and understand. It felt like someone had a sink plunger on the side of my head and popped something out of my head. I know it sounds bizarre but it actually happened. The meditation finished and the master Buddha asked if there was any feedback. I kept quiet as you can imagine what I was thinking if I told people what just happened to me. Anyway after a few people had commented he looked at me straight in the eye and said any feedback? So I thought *'what the hell'* and explained what had just happened and felt a bit stupid. He turned round to me and said *'I know you had hitchhiker.'* I knew immediately what he meant and then he proceeded to say that I'd had a dark energy attached to me and he had just removed it! Genny, who was with us, then went on to ask if I'd ever done the Ouija board to which I confirmed that I had in my thirties. I had actually communicated with my Granny Peg, which had been amazing but then unfortunately brought in a negative/evil energy which Genny said could have attached to me as I was open and sensitive at the time. This news didn't shock me and made perfect sense as I have always believed it is to do with the energies that surround us in this world. I then thought back to when we did this and then it dawned on me that 3 months later I had a massive psychotic episode back in 2003 where I thought I could stop a train. Everything then fell into place, the last bit of the puzzle. I am so grateful for what the master Buddha and Genny did for me that day and yes it might sound totally out there but it makes you think though. I 100% believe this because I have lived experience. I wonder how many other people have gone through what I have gone through but don't share it, as people will think they have lost the plot? Perhaps there is actually more to this world than what meets the eye? I am sure of it. So as I said before I believe it is a combination of my childhood trauma and not speaking out, partly chemical imbalance and the energies that surround us. I encourage people to share and talk about their experiences, don't do what I did and keep it all inside and then let it explode. I promise you that if you do, there are people out there willing to listen and not judge and believe me you are not alone.

In July, I became a published author through a charity book I was involved in – Courage: Stories Of Darkness To Light. I was one of eleven authors to share my true story of my mental health journey and all of the funds raised are supporting the work of The Samaritans.

We all face challenges in life and it boils down to how you approach and deal with them. You can either let it take over your life, have an adverse effect and bring you down, or you can brush yourself down, change your mindset and think positively. I don't know whether I will experience another episode in the future but I am not letting this affect my life. I believe you should cherish each day and enjoy life to the full. Stop worrying about the past as you can't change it, try to stop analysing everything and don't worry about the future. Remain in the now as much as possible because believe me if you do you might even experience things that you never knew existed. We live in a magical world and even though I have been through what I have been through I know that the best is yet to come. Peace, love & Harmony X

13

Kate's Story: Where had my sister gone?

I'm not sure when Liz's struggles started and whether it was gradual or much quicker, I just noticed something wasn't quite right. Before her first episode her life had taken on some changes, she had split from a long-term boyfriend and moved in with a friend, decided to have a nose operation and at work she had an incredibly bullying line manager, so she was living with some very stressful situations. What I know and remember very well is the phone call from her, it was not like my sister to be like how she was and I wondered what on earth the matter was.

'Can you come to the doctors with me' Liz sobbed. I replied 'Of course I can, let me know timings and I'll pick you up'.

Things hadn't been right over the last couple of weeks, Liz had become very insecure and agitated and increasingly upset most of the time. Focusing on work was becoming a challenge and very stressful so it didn't come as a great surprise that she needed to go to the doctors to see what he might suggest. After a 10 minute conversation Liz came out with a prescription of Prozac and the Doctor sent her on her way.

Over the next few weeks Liz's mood slowly improved, she took two weeks off of work but on her return she found her work was still very stressful and the bullying continued. At the time Liz and I worked at the same company and her line manager was, how can I put it politely, something of a bitch and had not only Liz on her radar but a few other people within the company, and by this point they had already left because of her. I certainly had been upset by her on a few occasions - that said Liz seemed to be doing OK. Things started to crank up for me as I had a new promotion, and was planning my wedding for that July so you could say I took my eye off the ball with regards to Liz, but things did seem to be looking up and she was improving.

Liz had lots going on and the Doctors' appointment now seemed a distant memory. I noticed on a few occasions she was a little hyper but Liz was always a little excitable so this didn't seem to be to out of the ordinary. She was always coming out with obscure and random quotes or sayings so I didn't think anything of it.

Around this time at work, I was planning a trip to Hixon to help set up the promotions team there, I came into contact with Liz a lot at work at this point as she was Operations manager so she sorted out my transport and the logistical side of the trip. Her mood had improved and it was great, if anything a little too great. Things seemed a little strange, is the best way to describe it, she was telling people how to best improve their lives, it was all very positive but to some people it was coming across very arrogant and as though they were being dictated to. In her advice she described herself as Jesus' sister and that she knew all what was going to happen. She mentioned winning the lottery and meeting Robbie Williams, it all seemed surreal at the time and just another funny story from Liz, albeit quite *"out there"*. Liz was always a bit off the wall so this seemed a bit odd but nothing too out of the ordinary so I or the family never questioned it.

I remember on one of our car share journeys home she was chatting away, criticizing my life and telling me what I should do about it, unfortunately this then caused a row as I objected and told her she was being quite rude. Previously if this had happened she normally would have apologized for over stepping the mark and that would be that, but she didn't, in fact she blatantly said she didn't care she had upset me and that what she was saying was right, so there! This was so out of character but still I didn't think there was anything majorly wrong. I have to say I was a little taken aback and the rest of the car journey home was quiet. The next few days I tried to let it go, I had a lot on and was now on my way to Hixon.

Mum called to say have a good trip and she'd catch up with me when I was back, she mentioned Liz was being very excitable and she was finding it wearing, I mentioned the row but we didn't discuss it much. Mum said that Liz was like a Duracell bunny and didn't know when to stop.

I was about an hour and half into my journey and I had to pull over at a services as I had a call come in from work, as I parked up, the phone went again and I answered, it was my Managing Director which was weird as if it was anything to do with the latest project I would generally get a call from my line manager or if plans had changed from Liz. My heart was in my mouth as I could immediately sense something was wrong. I started to feel sick and came over all hot and my palms started to sweat. Our Managing director calmly told me that my sister was asked to leave work and that my parents were asked to come and collect her. By this point my head was spinning and I started to ask myself all sorts of questions, why on earth were my parents coming to get her if she's upset again I'm sure she would be able to drive over to them? The Director explained that Liz had come into work smelling of alcohol and had been so hyper active that they suspected she was having a break down. I couldn't believe my ears, the next few minutes seemed like a blur. I said to him I would continue up to Hixon for the few days as planned and speak to my parents when I arrived. I wish now I had turned back and gone home because what happened over the next few days I really should have been there to support my parents. But hindsight is always an amazing thing.

Mum called briefly to fill me in but was terribly upset and didn't really tell me the whole story. I explained I had been to the Doctors with Liz and gave Mum all the Doctor's details and she put the phone down. It took me a while for things to sink in and I was still not entirely sure what had happened so I drove home the next day and left early to beat the traffic. When I got home and after Mark my husband explained the events, I never even realized the magnitude of what had happened, there was so much to take in. My step dad Trevor was very good and supported mum as much as possible at this difficult and life changing time.

Apparently Liz didn't just think she was like Jesus's sister she actually said she WAS and that she would prove it by stopping a train and was saying for us not to worry as she would be resurrected and her disciples would help her. I was in total shock and confused. Mark said Liz had been taken up to the mental hospital and she was completely out of control saying all kinds of weird stuff and it took 4 staff to hold her down and medicate her. She remained in hospital that night but I don't think she actually knew what was happening according to Mum who had left her there.

Liz was sectioned under the Mental Health Act and after a full assessment by a number of Doctors she was diagnosed with Bipolar Disorder 1 and Psychosis, and medicated up to the eyeballs. The next few weeks just seemed a complete blur of '*what the hell just happened*' my poor mum went into melt down herself which affected her health and the family all tried to rally round to pop up and visit. My step dad tried to keep everything calm and all together for the rest of the family but he was struggling just like the rest of us. It was a complete and utter life changing experience and came out of the blue. We were all just extremely thankful that Liz hadn't tried to stop the train and that the Managing director had acted quickly and addressed the situation. If it wasn't for him and calling our parents Liz wouldn't be here today as apparently according to Mum and Mark she had lost complete rationalization of her mind and was totally convinced that she had super powers and would be resurrected. It was so terrifying and very upsetting.

I was also a few weeks off getting married and I know this sounds terribly selfish but I really wanted my sister there to enjoy it with me, she was my chief bridesmaid and my best friend, I was absolutely mortified. We as a family had never ever witnessed or experienced anything like this before and it was frightening and unknown.

Liz was sectioned and in hospital for around 4 weeks, her Doctor agreed that she could pop out for the day to come to my wedding but that she was to be back in hospital straight after. So her dress was altered as by this time as she had lost so much weight and we were told all to watch her like a hawk and if there were any changes in her mood we were to drive her back to the secure unit straight away. I have pictures but you can see in her face she wasn't there, she was highly medicated and like a zombie, she doesn't really remember anything, which is such a shame as I know she would have really enjoyed it. Mark and I enjoyed our day but ever mindful of Liz and her Bipolar, we had a free bar at the wedding but asked everyone to donate to the mental health charity (Mind) as the team at the hospital had been brilliant and so supportive with her.

I went to visit Liz a few times before I went off on honey moon, but I have to say I struggled, the whole place just filled me with dread and I know how terrible that sounds but it just seemed utter chaos in there and I didn't feel in control. The patients were following Liz round like the pied piper and wouldn't leave her alone. It was awful and I truly felt for my poor sister. She was comatosed most of the time and I felt so helpless and upset. One particular visit stands out, Liz had been highly medicated and her jaw was clamping and gurning and she was almost struggling to speak, I couldn't help think to myself *'what the hell have they done to my sister!'* The hospital staff quickly gave her something to counter act the medication and then we chatted for a bit. I gave her a big hug, left and cried all the whole way home. The tears wouldn't stop and I felt drained and exhausted when I eventually got home. We went off on our honeymoon and when Liz was discharged she moved in with Mum and Trev, as whilst we were away she was not able to go home, according to the hospital, and look after herself. Liz had sunk into a deep depression. I phoned mum as much as I could and she was incredibly teary and stressed, Liz was extremely low and lying in bed all day, not eating and mentioning she didn't want to live anymore, my poor mum was devastated.

Over the next few months I tried to get back into work, Liz and I worked at the same company and attitudes towards me, and her had changed. People in the team were OK and some were supportive but there was definitely a lack of understanding of Liz's condition. Management were intolerant, uncomfortable and had a big lack of understanding, they didn't even try to find out more information, or how to go about dealing with her in the best way. After 10 months at home, Liz came back to work for a bit but walked out not long after, she just couldn't handle the atmosphere and apparently the bullying had started again. I left shortly after as I found the whole experience upsetting. I couldn't cope with their lack of trying to understand her condition and her bullying line manager and the way she was treated. I believe they dealt with the whole situation in a discriminatory way, so I left. I now looked to go back into my original profession and skill-set, which is hairdressing.

I continued to support Liz in every way I could although I struggled emotionally and had a lack of understanding myself but I tried my best to learn more. I read books to help and I visited her doctors with her when I could. I was pregnant now with my first child Sophie and dealing with both Liz and hormones I have to say was a struggle. She had times where she would show signs of mania again, I would plead with her to try and listen to her doctors, not to drink and take care of herself to help as it was stressing me and the baby out but she would just say *'don't worry I will bring you and your baby back to life.'* It was incredibly hard to deal with and I didn't always want to be around her as she was so unpredictable.

Over the next year or so there were many moments of mania and she would wander into town and meet up with loads of strange groups of people, making unlikely friends with people we had never heard of. Spending all afternoons in the pub and talking about all the things she was going to do. At one point she come to live with us for 6 months and stress levels in my marriage hit an all-time high as Liz spiralled into another mini episode. I remember one morning waking up about 4am with a sense something wasn't quite right, I popped in to check on my daughter who was then around 5 months old and she wasn't in bed, I went into an immediate panic and rushed down stairs to find my sister outside sitting in the garden with Sophie. I tried to calm myself as best I could and asked Liz why she was up so early. Her response was *'I couldn't sleep, so I woke Sophie up to show her the sunrise'* she said just like that as if it was the norm.

I class them as mini episodes but in truth they all feel like they blended into one - this was the new Liz that we were all struggling to come to terms with. The eccentric highs were at times unbearable and the lows were draining and we were all left wondering how to help. The full blown episodes were when she lost her rational mind and would become a danger to herself and others, this would be when we would have to involve the police as she wouldn't voluntarily go to the hospital, these were the times she was sectioned. I decided to do a course at hospital for people that were in the same situation as me. The course was really helpful in lots of ways, the staff at the hospital were amazing and really knew their stuff, I did find however some of the sessions were taken up with people just wanting to tell their story which was fine but I felt that was more of group therapy rather than hard core facts about what we were dealing with. If I'm honest, I wasn't tolerant of anyone else's story at that point as I just wanted to know how to help Liz and I needed clear cut defining facts on how to do that. Over the course I realized that the stories that were shared were important to each of us, as we all had common themes, things that we could all be aware of if one of our loved ones was going into an episode.

I learnt very early on that all I could do was support Liz, not try and control her or her Bipolar or not force her to try different things - that was for the professionals. To just listen and let her make her own choices, even though certainly in times of episode and mania that resulted in spending lots of money and actions I didn't agree with. One manic episode included booking 2 limos up to London to search the streets for Robbie Williams as he was in town, and have lunch at the Ivy with him, luckily we were able to find the information and cancel the bookings and the company was very understanding. There are loads more examples that I could share all completely different and frightening.

There were times when Liz was sectioned and had to go back into the hospital, and she would cause mayhem, she would be Jesus's sister and rally her disciples and try and get them out of the hospital. She was placed on a secure unit with 5-10 min checks but that still didn't stop Liz. We had a phone call around 9pm one evening to say she had escaped and we were to bring her back if she made contact. That night she made her way to a mutual friends' house, she must have walked over about 3 fields and a mile or so to get there, the police were called and back she went. It was a constant worry about what was going to happen next and Liz just didn't seem to be helping herself. How she managed to escape though is beyond me as the hospitals are supposed to be secure units which is worrying. One of her episodes which is now engrained on everyone's memory as it was so threatening and negative and was probably one of the scariest moments of my life and I learnt a very valuable lesson that day.

14

What A Whirlwind

Liz turned up at my house unannounced with her current boyfriend, he looked petrified. Liz was talking crazily and jumping around and wouldn't sit still, she was talking about angels and demons and that the demons were coming to get her. I had seen her wound up like this before but never this scared or aggressive in her behaviour. It wasn't aimed at anyone but she was saying some pretty scary stuff. My husband is one of the most laid back people you could find but even he seemed rattled. Liz was threatening to hurt the children and kept looking up and talking to some invisible being and saying I will beat you. Mark rang the hospital as this was now 3am in the morning and none of us had slept, they couldn't help as they needed 2 doctors to be able to come out and assess Liz, we were all frustrated, angry and desperate as there seemed to be no help available and they didn't advise us what to do. This was an extreme concern and we were surprised that the hospital didn't help us.

We soldiered on for another couple of hours and tried to the best of our abilities to keep Liz calm. At 6am things took a big turn for the worst. I have always constantly been around in Liz's life and always felt I was able to handle anything her Bipolar could throw at me. My naivety cost me, as there was an unforgettable turn of events. Whilst we were upstairs in the bedroom, Liz suddenly turned on me, she called me Myra Hindley and screamed that I was going to attack her children (my daughters). Sophie was just under 3 and Ella was a babe, she grabbed Ella from my arms and luckily gave her to her current boyfriend, then she pushed and shoved me and shouted in my face. I was in a state of shock and didn't know what to do. Her boyfriend had locked himself in the main bathroom with my youngest screaming, so I was relieved that had happened.

Liz suddenly then turned and ran out of the room and proceeded to bang on the locked door of the bathroom where then her boyfriend was hiding. In the meantime, Sophie my eldest had sneaked downstairs to find Daddy in the garage phoning the police, after being pushed over, I then ran into my toilet and locked the door as I was utterly scared out of my wits and didn't know what Liz was capable of, it was like she was possessed and all hell had let loose.

Liz then ran downstairs out of the door screaming up the road and continued running until she reached the local store of Tesco's, shouting that I had taken her kids and that I was going to kill them and please call the police. The police were already on their way and Liz was detained at the local Tesco by a gentleman who had her in a head lock, as she thought his child was the devil child. Mark and I arrived and witnessed this and it was incredibly dramatic and so very distressing. Our family was shocked and knocked side-ways, Liz was taken in and once again sectioned. I think I probably cried for a week after this episode, it was so frightening and I had let Liz down and my family too and I had put my kids in danger and I was only trying to help. I would never make that mistake again as the risk was too high. I spent the next 6 months having nightmares about that day, it was horrendous and one that I would never ever want to repeat again.

I also felt incredibly guilty that I wasn't able to do more. My friends were brilliant, however I did have one friend whom didn't show the same level of understanding. I was devastated after I confided in what I thought was a close friend at the time but was soon to learn how it felt to know sanism, something, which I will mention later in more depth.

Things took a while to calm down, Liz's boyfriend ended their relationship and Liz found this difficult and upsetting, he just couldn't cope with her condition. I understood at the time as I just wanted to grab the kids, my husband and move as far away as possible, but that's no way to deal with it. I didn't visit Liz at all after this episode. I have to be honest I was never particularly good at the visiting, the other patients at the hospital scared me. Also the way Liz seemed to behave in hospital just made me feel so uncomfortable however my levels of understanding have improved now and I have become much more patient with others. The next few months were very strained and draining. After this particular episode Liz and I were now not as close. I struggled with how this episode had caused upset with my family and that both my children had become involved. I was worried that my relationship with Liz wouldn't recover from this one and it made me feel incredibly sad and empty.

It's really difficult at times as I have been ashamed of how I felt, I would often during Liz's difficult episodes feel upset and angry that I was constantly being dragged into her latest episode, always feeling like I was the sister who had to cope all the time and remain strong. Over the years, we have had periods of time where we haven't spoken, due to arguments and disagreements mainly to do with her Bipolar and the fact that her brain works so differently from other people. I think it takes time to understand and after this particular episode, with having a spate of anxiety attacks myself and struggling to cope emotionally, I hope I have more appreciation for others, I'm not perfect but I will keep on trying.

As I mentioned earlier, I had my own little snippet of being judged, the friend whom I confided in turned all strange something I hadn't experienced before. At the time our children were at the same school, Liz was improving and as a family we were all desperately trying to get over this last years' terrible episode.

I had chats with staff at the hospital as how to deal with the situation and guidance on how we were all to get back on track. I was still very fearful of Liz around my kids but I was always encouraged not to separate her but to keep a watchful eye on the situation. My daughter's school was amazing, they knew that if Liz turned up unannounced she was not allowed to collect the kids at home time and I had to be called. Liz was to be explained the procedure re collection in a way that it would not upset her or make her feel she was in the wrong, the school were so supportive.

By this time Liz was out of the hospital with regular day visits and getting better by the day, she asked to come to one of the kids' church services. I spoke with Liz's doctor and we both felt this was a good time to start building bridges. That evening this friend/mum from the school phoned to say she had been to see the headmistress of the school and asked that Liz was not to be allowed to attend the church service or any school events. I firstly couldn't believe my ears at what she told me and also the fact she called me to let me know.

I have never known one of my friends be like this before, it was all very confusing, I had each step of the way reassured her that I would never ask my sister to something like this if I or her doctors felt she wasn't ready or the fact that she was a risk. Luckily the headmistress of the school was not a judgemental person and incredibly understanding. The friend in question continued to make her feelings known at other events, such as the school fête and sports day, it was almost like a witch hunt. Unfortunately because I had been open and honest with my sister about how this friend was feeling she declined to come along and it really upset Liz making her feel insecure and paranoid. It affected her confidence and she became withdrawn. I wished now I had never confided in that person nor told my sister what she had been like because to this day I think this is why it has taken so long for Liz to speak out for fear of others treating her this way and being judgemental towards her. This was a prime example of someone's ignorance of the condition and of the situation. Unfortunately, there was no improvement in her thinking and sadly we are no longer friends, so being a part of writing this book I hope that at least opinions may change. I don't expect people to not be upset by what can happen but to show some willingness and compassion, that would be helpful and perhaps gain more insight to people's condition and learn or educate themselves better. Moving forward I have learnt a great deal about Liz's condition and I'm sure there is still lots more to learn. I try to make sure I keep in constant contact with Liz as I believe this helps her to feel supported and connected.

Liz went on to meet her now partner Darell, and over the last few years we have been less directly involved with Liz's episodes due to Darell being so supportive in looking after Liz, that does not mean however we are not here for her. Their relationship has gone from strength to strength and although in the beginning Liz still had some tough episodes, with his and our support, it seems to have made their commitment together even stronger.

We continue to support her and Liz had a very minor blip about 4 years ago and because I was away on holiday I felt conscious that I was a long way away, so in order to make her feel we were there for her, I sent her pictures nearly every day and the girls face timed her whenever possible. We wanted to know we were there for support and of course to let her know that she is very much loved always!

I am incredibly proud of how Liz handles herself and how she doesn't let her condition define her and that she has turned some somewhat negative times into positive ones to help others in their struggle with mental health.

Here is something I wrote when remembering all that we have been through.

My Whip Up

I've told her I'm OK but she thinks I'm going high again....
I wish she'd just Listen

Looks like we are in for another episode I need her to see the doctor...
I wish she'd just Listen

I'm Jesus's sister so I can make anything come true I'll let the doc look at me but...
I wish she'd just Listen

Jesus's sister oh no not that one again, did Jesus even have a sister grrrrrrrrrrrrr...
I wish she'd just Listen

I've decided I will lead my disciples out of this Centre and into the open I told her, set them free...
I wish she'd just Listen

"I've had a phone call Mark, the hospital again she tried to escape with 12 others this time"...
I wish she'd just Listen

They've given me medication I feel out of it and I can hardly speak good job my disciples understand me, they listen but........
I wish she'd just Listen

So much medication, her mouth is all funny she's totally out of it I can't help...
She can't even hear me

I hate this place I know I'm not Jesus' sister anymore, please let me out of here
No-one is listening to me...

Now in 2019, moving on from where we were such a long time ago at Liz's first episode in 2003, some things seem to have progressed. I'm still learning about how best to help Liz and her last episode in 2018 I managed to overcome my anxiety and fear of being in the hospital with her and managed to visit and support her much more. Liz only had to stay in hospital for three days which is a marked improvement and we were desperate to get her out of there because the environment was horrendous and was making her worse. This is where I believe mental health has not improved. I remember the hospital back in 2003, they were incredibly supportive although I still felt uncomfortable, but now it seems to have deteriorated and the staff are rushing about with paperwork and have no time for the patients. People who are in there seemed to have no support and there seems to be a desperate lack of staff. I never felt comfortable going into the mental hospital as sometimes things could kick off but I always had a sense that it could be handled, this time however I felt very vulnerable. Liz and I have recently gone into NHS Essex Partnership Unit Trust and have spoken about our experiences. Liz has spoken about her experience with regards to being a patient and mine from a family support perspective. The staff were new recruits into the trust, and we believed this would help benefit the staff and give them a better understanding. Liz and I do a lot of voluntary work however we can't always take time off work and we know it is so important to get the message across and educate people. Raising awareness is brilliant but the hospitals around the country, I believe are in desperate need of help and support from the government.

I currently am involved with Made for More charity group and I'm realizing more and more every day that support is important. I also volunteer as a mentor in schools to help teenagers deal with general life and quite often there are cases where children have had to be signposted to a mental health team. I think the fact is that the awareness is more prevalent now but needs more people helping and talking about their mental health. The schools' families are all trying to make the greatest of efforts to improve the stigma attached to mental health. It's widely more accepted now and I'm hoping and praying this will continue to improve. Every day by creating awareness whilst educating and conducting talks in schools, at events and the NHS, Liz and I are hoping that eventually these types of hospital facilities will improve and also there will be reduced stigma and discrimination with regards to mental health. I want the world to be a better place for our children and Liz speaking out like she does makes people feel they are not alone and have some hope.

15

Mum's Story: Do we ever stop worrying about our daughters?

2003 was both a happy and very stressful year. The joy emanated from my younger daughter Kate's marriage, the excitement and anticipation of a joyous day greatly anticipated.

Unfortunately, a couple of months before this event, my elder daughter Liz began showing serious signs of unusual behaviour. She had a few months before had depression and ended a difficult long-term relationship. Subsequent to leaving her boyfriend, she lived with a girlfriend and started a wild alcoholic party lifestyle. This together with a stressful job and serious bullying at work literally *'blew her mind.'*

At the time I was working with a Housing Association who cared for people with Learning Difficulties and Mental Health. To a degree I had some insight into mental health problems and when Liz was diagnosed, I had good support from my colleagues at work.

Liz's Bipolar manifested itself in extremely erratic behaviour, talking quickly and forcibly with her sheer force of personality being incredibly stressful and wearing. She was very delusional, had very grandiose ideas about who she was and what she could achieve. Terrifying really, as she was a danger to herself and possibly others. We only realized the full extent when we picked her up from work after the Managing director urgently rang us and expressed his concern. We took Liz to the doctor and she deteriorated rapidly and had to be admitted to the Psychiatric Unit. Liz was jumping up and down saying she wanted to change the world and that no-one was listening to her. This in itself was extremely difficult as Liz would not accept there was anything wrong, which finally resulted in her being forcibly injected to calm her down. During the following days Liz was very doped up and zombie like but at least she was controllable. She remained in hospital for a month and was finally released under the care of me, and my husband. She was now very depressed and was equally a danger to herself. She would lie on the bed for hours just gazing out of the window and remaining motionless not eating or drinking. Fortunately she was smoking at the time and this saved the day in as much as it necessitated her going outside so at least she moved. It was difficult to get her to eat but with gentle persuasion and oodles of patience she gradually improved. This part of her condition was very serious and it was totally important that she had us to look after her otherwise she would just have wasted away; on the positive side with the depression we knew where she was and she was quiet! All in all, it took ten months to balance Liz's equilibrium, to get her medication correct and for her to return to work.

Life has to change dramatically when you have Bipolar. A much calmer, quieter lifestyle is required and for a number of years Liz did not accept this, which resulted in many episodes of manic behaviour. Bipolar does not get better; it is a condition that can be managed via medication and careful living but the high life, stressful job, drinking etc just negates the medication and the mind spirals into a manic episode.

One of the major problems we found during these very difficult years was the support from Social Services was such a mess. There was no continuity, we never had the same Social Worker twice to deal with Liz, the left hand never knew what the right hand was doing and in the end we knew how best to deal with Liz rather than the supposed experts. However, when Liz eventually entered the Psychiatric Unit, the care she received there was very good. The staff were caring and extremely patient; I cannot thank them enough for the caring of Liz when she most needed it.

It is some 16 years we have experienced living around Bipolar. At times it has been so stressful, difficult, emotional and very worrying but Liz is more mature now, able to manage her Bipolar and, most important, she has the wonderful support of her caring, loving partner Darell. We so appreciate that he is there for Liz as it becomes increasingly difficult, as we get older, to deal with her condition.

Liz is very involved with supporting mental health issues, giving talks and doing much to support those with mental health difficulties. She does take time out to escape to the country in her caravan with her beloved Darell and her two doting dogs and having calm gentle times to *counter* balance the rush and speed of modern day life.

I think that nowadays more people are talking out about their mental health, however this still needs to increase, too many people suffer in silence and I hope that the fact my daughter has spoken her truth that it makes a difference and gives people the confidence to share their experiences too. We need to make this world a better place for our children.

16

Sophie and Ella's Story: Auntie Lizzie

Back in 2008, I was 3 and Ella was 1 so we don't remember much but what I do remember is a very scary episode that our Auntie Lizzie had. She burst through the bedroom door and just started shouting at Mum. I was so scared and ran out of the room to find Dad who was downstairs. All I was thinking at the time was it looked like some-one else was in her head and controlling her and making her do some horrible and nasty things to Mum. I don't know what happened afterwards and all I know is that Auntie Lizzie had been taken to hospital to get better. I was so confused at the time and really didn't know what was going on but this was my first experience of what I found out later was a condition called Psychosis. A few years later Auntie Lizzie had another episode and she came round to our house not long after she had been discharged from hospital. We both remember she was extremely hyper and jumping up and down on the sofa and couldn't sit still. This was so out of character for her although I know she was happy, but not this excitable. She was obviously recovering from another manic episode but still a little high. I felt helpless and couldn't help her. I didn't really understand what was happening and neither did Ella. We were still so confused again so asked Mum to explain in more detail about Auntie Lizzie's condition and Mum did extremely well. It was still very scary and upsetting to see our Auntie going through this and couldn't imagine what she was going through.

We don't know how to make it better as we are not sure how to help and lack understanding of the condition. We learnt a bit when Mum explained it, perhaps if we both knew how to help we could offer some support. We couldn't relate to it as we have never experienced it, so it is really hard to understand.

I have someone at school that suffers from mental health and I constantly encourage her to talk to someone and not hold it inside. It is so important to talk out and share what you are going through. You then realize that there are other people out there that do suffer too.

It seems like in the world today there are more people who are suffering and going through similar things to our Auntie Lizzie, more people need to be educated and understand what people are going through. We think that doing talks in schools is great so pupils can learn from lived experience and realize they are not alone.

I was bullied at school. The girls made me feel worthless, irritated and I was annoyed that they could upset me so much. I told Mum everything and she really helped me. So it's good to share and talk about it. Ella was bullied too and she deals with things in her head or writes things down to help her. She felt angry too and wanted in her mind to do things to the bullies but never did anything physical - it was just her way of dealing with it. If someone was being bullied at our school now we would encourage them to either tell the teacher or tell their parents but not keep it inside as that is the worst thing you can do. Don't suffer in silence, it messes with your head and makes you feel even worse.

At school now we both have a sense of freedom and have great friends that we can talk to. We can only say to people don't let your emotions build up and don't be afraid to cry and let things out. It shows you are human and it makes you feel better.

Our message to people reading this book is to make sure you take medication, which helps and also to find a way of expressing how you feel. So it really is what works for you, as everyone is different.

Ella also feels there needs to be better support in hospitals as Auntie Lizzie's experience, especially her recent admissions have not been good and some of the staff have not been supportive. It would be good to extend the visiting hours for family and friends and let the patient know that her family are there supporting them on the outside as I know Auntie Lizzie feels very alone when she is in hospital.

We both feel it's great that Auntie Lizzie copes well with her condition and doesn't let it bring her down. She does loads for charity and also does talks, which we think is excellent. We would like her to come and talk at our school because we think that would really help. She is so open and honest with us and other people and is not embarrassed to talk about it in order to help other people, which is really nice.

We are both so proud of our Auntie Lizzie and she still maintains a smile on her face even though she has been through some seriously rough times. We love her very much and will always support her in what she does and will continue to encourage other people to share their emotions and offer support where we can. As they say a problem shared is a problem solved.

17
Glynis's Story: Workplace

Over the last couple of months, we had been struggling to find an administrator at work. I tasked Vanessa to get some more potential candidates in for interview and prepare a test for them. There was one particular girl that was short-listed and Vanessa convinced me to see her. As soon as I met Liz we gelled instantly, we had the same personality and she made me laugh and vice versa. I enjoyed talking to Liz and she made me feel very relaxed and I knew that I would be able to trust her, which is so important to the relationship between a manager and a personal assistant. Liz had been offered another job at the same time but I was determined to employ her so I rang her up and managed to persuade her to come and work for our company. It took a while for HR to be on-board with Liz, but she started on a temporary contract in November 2012.

After a few months of working at the company, Liz came into my office looking very sheepish and concerned, saying that she had something extremely important to tell me, and it was a bit embarrassing. I wondered what on earth it was and for some reason thought she might tell me that she used to be a man. When I told Liz this she laughed and said you would be the only person that would think of that and then said she was Bipolar. I was surprised but for me it didn't make any difference; Liz was Liz and did a great job. I was extremely naïve and didn't know fully what it meant. I didn't realise that the episodes could come and go and I thought that everything was under control. Liz explained the details and said that she'd had episodes in the past and told me about the warning signs. My office overlooked the garden, and at one point I looked outside and it was raining over the large tree but not the other side of the garden, I pointed this out to Liz and we both burst out laughing, it was surreal but it broke the ice.

It was the following year and I was on business in New York and even before I went, Liz seemed very up and down and active. I got a phone call from Liz in the middle of the night, she was talking very quickly and seemed rather wired. Liz said *'have you seen the news about Hyderabad bringing Barclays Bank down'* and said something about fraud. I didn't know what she was talking about and was still half asleep. Liz said that; *'we have people that come from Hyderabad in our work, they might be planning something.'* I tried to reassure her and then put the phone down and went back to sleep. Thinking at the time it was a bit odd but I would sort things out in the morning as I was flying back the next day.

When I got back to the office, I found out that Liz had been saying that she was getting weird emails and that one of her colleagues eyes were piercing blue and they clearly weren't. It was all a bit worrying so I sent Liz home to take some time out. Darell rang me the next day saying he had taken Liz to the doctors and she was slightly hyper and he was planning to take her away camping to calm her down a bit. I personally didn't think that this was the best thing to do but Darell knows Liz better so I left Liz in his hands.

I spent the whole weekend researching about Bipolar and mental health so I could find out all about it and what the symptoms and signs were. The more I read the more I understood the condition and that Liz was definitely showing the symptoms.

Liz unfortunately that night went into a manic episode and ended up being sectioned in the local hospital. We looked after Boris so Darell could concentrate on Liz. I got involved also in Liz's care and went to the mental hospital twice to visit Liz to see how she was. Before that I had never entered a mental hospital in my life and I was taken back with the atmosphere and patients. It made the film *'The one who flew over the cuckoo's nest'* seem real and it reminded me of this film. It really upset me with all the different issues that the patients had, from self-harm to one guy who seemed normal until he started talking to a tree about the drugs baron. There was also one lady that was so highly medicated that her face was swollen from all the drugs and it thoroughly upset me. She looked tortured and I can still see her face in my mind today. It was unbelievable and Liz seemed so normal compared to everyone else and I just wanted her out of there as soon as possible. When I came to leave I couldn't get out as I had to wait for a staff member to open the door and it then hit me how vulnerable I was and that I was locked in and so was poor Liz. I attended Liz's outpatient appointment and spoke to the psychiatrist and got involved on Liz's advance decision, which is a document that states Liz's wishes whilst she is in hospital.

Liz took a month off work to recuperate and we were all totally supportive of her as we knew what a great job she did when she was well and why should she be penalized due to this unfortunate condition.

Liz had another 2 episodes whilst working for me but I managed to spot the signs so she avoided being sectioned, which were great. Liz increased her medication each time, which really helped her relax and sleep and we managed to get the home treatment team out to see her as soon as possible to support her through this time.

Liz was made redundant from Marsh in March 2018 and I had moved on to another job but I had heard that it didn't work out with the other company she had gone to as she'd had another episode at their place of work. I made it my mission to speak to Roy and see if the job was still available to be his personal assistant. Roy called Liz in for an interview and I was over the moon for her as knew how good she was at her job and so pleased when she got the job.

Liz started in June 2018 and seemed to be getting on well. In November I had Roy and Gabby from Liz's office pop down and see me to say that Liz had another episode and was in hospital. They looked concerned and asked for my advice and explained what had happened to the lead up. Liz had been on holiday to the Caribbean and Roy said that she seemed quite high from the holiday but he just put it down to the fact that she was still in holiday mode. I explained that the reason for the episode could have been the lack of sleep, different time zone and also medication at different times could all have an adverse effect on Liz. I offered my help and support and suggested different ways to help Liz in the future. I advised Roy to ring Darell as soon as he saw the signs in order to remove Liz from the workplace and gain some support and help. I also mentioned that it is difficult for Liz because being on a high is a great feeling and she really does not want it to end.

This has really opened my eyes to mental health and made me be more patient and understanding. Darell, Liz's partner is one in a million and is a great support to her however sometimes he doesn't want to see that it is happening to Liz as I know he is frightened of her going to hospital again.

I was upset for Liz as I know her sister didn't visit her for many years in hospital because of how scared the hospital made her feel. But I hear that during the last episode Kate visited Liz and I am so pleased she managed to face her fear and support Liz.

When I got back from visiting Liz I had her sick note in my hand, my husband said if we had the puppy for another three weeks he may join Liz as he had found Boris picking up the cats bed with the cat still in it earlier.

On one visit to outpatients with Liz, a lady with no legs in a wheel chair started swearing at me because I was in office attire, I was mortified but ignored it, I felt really horrible. With a physical health condition you wouldn't think twice about going to visit someone in hospital so why should it be any different for people with mental health conditions. I suppose it's the lack of understanding that is why this book is so important to educate people.

It's been a massive learning curve for me and I am so proud to work for a company that supports people with mental health conditions. I have been on the radio with Liz to educate and support people going through difficulties and think it's great that our company offered

Liz stability when she was going through her episodes. Due to the companies support and our understanding of this condition we have maintained an excellent employee who is great at her job.

It is a very important message to get across that you need to be there for them in the same way you are when someone has physical symptoms or an issue. Everyone has their own mental problem, because there are days when sometimes you don't feel very enthusiastic and can't be bothered and some days when you are happier than normal. We all suffer in one way, or another and should think what that would be like multiplied a hundred times, with what Liz has gone through and others do too.

18

Darell's Story: Life changer

I saw Liz from across the street, she hadn't changed a bit and was looking mighty fine. I hadn't seen her for about 10 years, so we decided to go for a catch up and a coffee. I knew Liz from way back about twenty years ago from going out and about in Chelmsford. We chatted about the old times and Liz told me all what had recently happened to her. She had recently split up from her boyfriend and this had really upset her as he didn't fully understand her Bipolar and it had scared him. I was actually quite surprised that this had happened and why he didn't support her, but then again I didn't know the full story at that point and I suppose we are all different in how we react. I didn't realise that Liz had been diagnosed with Bipolar and felt a bit sorry for her but also didn't really understand what it was myself either. Liz was living round at her friend Karen's at the time and I had a spare room available, which was nearer to the town centre and I wanted to look after Liz too. I felt that she'd had a rough time and I suppose I felt I could fix it and offer her support. I had just come out of a bad relationship too and was not looking for another one so just wanted to help Liz out. The last thing I wanted was to go into a relationship with Liz, that was the furthest thought from my mind. I was not in a good place so needed to sort myself out first. However we did become FB's - If people know what that means! I was still drinking and going out partying. I do remember trying to show off once and doing a somersault on the bed, I hit it so hard it broke and we were both in hysterics. We decided to go to Cuba for us to try and bond a bit more. It was an odd holiday as we were both a bit unsure of how we felt, however we enjoyed the break and the sunshine.

When we got back, Liz decided that I wasn't the one for her so we ended the FB relationship. I was gutted as I had genuinely started to get feelings for Liz. Liz moved back into the spare room again and I started to go out more regularly on the piss. Liz started seeing a guy called Patrick and I was extremely jealous but I was determined to win Liz back, so I cut down my drinking and started going to the gym on a regular basis. I felt much better and my physique improved dramatically. I was going to show her!

Liz went to Portugal with Patrick and when she got back she didn't seem overly happy and was very impressed about how I had turned myself around. We decided to make a go of it and start a relationship. I know that her sister and Mark her husband were not overly keen to begin with as they were extremely protective over Liz and I must admit I was a bit of a bad boy in my past, but I was hoping that things would change when they saw that I cared and would look after Liz.

I got rid of the flat and we both moved into Liz's place in Boreham, it was only a one bedroomed place but we loved it. Liz bought a kitten called Bobbie, a fluffy long haired black cat. He was adorable and soon became our little friend. We also bought an Audi A4 Convertible which was our first car together and also went on a lot of camping trips. We had bought a big Berghaus tent so virtually every weekend we used to just get in the car and go off camping. It was great.

I used to still go out every Friday and drank quite heavily which I know that Liz didn't like. We used to have arguments over this as Liz said I changed into a complete knob - those are her words!

There was one time Liz was became increasingly argumentative, even more than normal and she seemed to be very agitated. She brought up about the past, my drinking and accused me of doing drugs. We went to bed that night and during the night she woke up and started chopping the air and kick-boxing the air. When I asked her what she was doing, she said she was fighting the aliens and chopping their heads off with a samurai sword. I was totally shocked and thought this girl has totally lost the plot, it also frightened me as I wasn't sure what to do. I didn't know whether to call her mum, sister, the police, my mind was racing of all the different possibilities. I just kept thinking what the hell is going on here. Liz had got a bottle of alien perfume that she wore and said that this was the alien baby and we had to give it back to the Alien King. I went along with it as I didn't want to make things worse as Liz had clearly lost her mind. Liz then wanted to go and see the doctor so jumped in the car, I went with her as I was not driving at that point. We started to have a heated argument, as she was driving all over the place and she stopped on the verge of the A12 and basically screamed at me to get out, so I did and she just drove off. I didn't know what was happening; I didn't know where she was going, or what she was capable of. I didn't know what to expect as had never been in this position before and didn't have a clue how to handle Liz. In hindsight I should have taken the keys from her and hidden them but it all happened so quickly and I think I was in shock.

The next time I saw Liz was at the park and ride in Chelmsford, I had rung the police after Liz had driven off and they advised me that they had tracked her down to there. I got Michael, one of my close friends to pick me up and we rushed down there. Liz was surrounded by police when I arrived and she was saying that her feet were stuck to the floor with super glue and she couldn't move. Liz flipped when she saw me so I hung back a bit. Liz just wouldn't move although the police said that if she did, she would be detained. After about an hour the school kids were leaving a nearby bus and they were all staring at Liz and for some reason she went to grab one of them. As soon as she did this, the police grabbed her and detained her in handcuffs. She was put in the back of the car and rushed to the hospital for an assessment. I felt mortified and wondered whether I could have done more to stop this happening. I was still in shock and the police told me to go back and get some rest. Trev (Liz's step dad) was there at the park and ride and I went back to Liz's mums and told them what had happened and asked what the normal procedure was. They filled me in so I would be prepared if there was a next time. I wasn't allowed to see Liz for the first 24 hours and it never even crossed my mind to leave her in this desperate state. She needed my support so I packed a few clothes for her after speaking to her parents then went to visit Liz at the hospital the next day with her Mum.

I felt intimidated in hospital and I don't know how Liz coped with being in there. The staff were all busy with paperwork and Liz was on her own in a room. She looked so vulnerable and my heart went out to her. Her mum brushed her hair as it was all matted and spoke to her in a reassuring way. Liz was like a zombie and was obviously doped up with medication to calm her down. This time Liz was detained in the secure unit for a week and every day I bought her £20 in change for the phone and cigarettes as she had started smoking again. Each time I left I used to see her with all the boys in the hideaway puffing away and she would wave like a naughty school girl. I did find it amusing, not because she was locked away, that was horrific, but because she seemed to take it all in her stride and carry on as if nothing was wrong. When she came back she had time off work to recover and then went back to work after about 2 weeks. Her employers were fantastic and so supportive and allowed her to go back on a phased basis to help and support her.

We decided to buy another kitten for some reason and thought this would also help Liz after her turmoil and last episode. His name was Billy, and Bobbie and he used to fight like cat and dog! It was so funny to watch.

Liz was now back on a different medication and I was happy to keep an eye on her and her moods. She didn't really suffer from depression which surprised me as I thought that was what Bipolar was, fluctuating mood swings. Liz's episodes sounded more like Psychosis, as I did a bit of research to find out what the condition was all about. I decided to go to a Bipolar support group with Liz's mum to find out more information, I found this extremely interesting and it really helped me on how to cope now and in the future. I discovered that a lot of people were going through the same issues as we were, some even worse. There was one guy who was beside himself and didn't know what else to do to help his wife. It was so upsetting but it helped a great deal.

We went to Antigua for my 40th birthday, which was amazing, we met some lovely people from Wickford who we are still friends with. One night Liz grabbed the microphone off the rep and decided to express her undying love for me. All I kept thinking is *'what the fuck is she doing now!'* Who knows with Liz, she is a bit of a live wire. She asked me to marry her, I wasn't expecting that but was secretly over the moon and accepted. The rest of the night was like a whirl wind and so surreal. I think I am still in shock now and it's been 10 years!

The house in Boreham was getting too small especially with the two cats, so we decided to look elsewhere. We decided to rent the house out to one of the neighbour's friends. I did warn Liz that it would be a big mistake but she felt sorry for the girl so agreed to rent her the house for a year. We found a 2 bedroomed house in Witham so moved in within 3 months, I wasn't sure initially of the house but went with it as Liz said there was lots of potential. I started straight away, being the builder I am, as the house was not to my taste. I ripped all the kitchen cupboards off, stripped the carpets from the bedrooms, along with the wallpaper. I was on a mission to get things done! One of Liz's friends also gave us a great discount on a hot tub so we had one of these positioned in the back garden. During our time here Liz had changed jobs and now was working as a care coordinator looking after adults with learning difficulties, which she found highly challenging and difficult. I supported her through this financially and physically along with looking after the house.

One day I remember coming home and Liz came out of the house saying how much she loved me. Instinctively I knew she was up to something and immediately thought she had bought a dog. Not sure why I thought that but Liz was very impulsive sometimes. I told her that she could take the dog back as I wasn't interested! Although, when I saw the little puppy on the sofa my heart melted. He was the most adorable little thing ever and he was a springer spaniel, something I had wanted since I was young. We named him Boris and obviously he never got returned!

So we had Boris, Bobbie and Billy in the family! All was looking well, I must admit I did have my ups and downs in my life and things weren't all rosy. I had always had problems with my dad so these haunted me sometimes and dampened my mood. I also started having counselling for my anxiety and anger management at a private hospital through Liz's work, which really helped. Liz was pleased with this as it was putting a strain on our relationship and I must admit if it wasn't for her pushing me I probably would still have many nightmares about it now. I am not saying I don't but they are less frequent. Liz had moved jobs as she acknowledged that care work was not for her, although I did respect her for sticking with it for a year and dealing with the vulnerable people, however it was not in her nature and she was too impatient. Liz got herself a personal assistant job for an insurance company in Witham, about 10 minutes' walk away. Perfect location so I was happy.

Everything seemed to be going well and we had just recently come back from Las Vegas, love that place. Liz seemed a bit stressed at work and her mood was heightened but I didn't think much of it. Liz is an extremely spiritual person, however when she becomes unwell she starts talking non-stop about spirits/energies and can feel them all around her. She was talking a bit too much about them for my liking and becoming agitated again, this sent warning signs to me so I kept a close eye on her.

One night she didn't sleep very well as she said she felt negative energy around her, I took her to the doctors the next day but they said she was OK, as the day went on, Liz became increasingly worse so I rang the crisis team. I advised them about her condition and said that it escalated pretty quickly. They wanted to speak to Liz so I passed the phone over. Liz said that she thought aliens were on the planet to which they replied *'well a lot of people think that'* and as she wasn't suicidal didn't think it was an emergency so we booked an appointment the next day with the psychiatrist.

I decided the best thing or what I thought was the best thing was to take Liz and Boris away camping for the night just to get some peace and quiet and relax. This was the biggest mistake I made to what happened next.

19

A Turn of Events

We all went off to the camping site at Mersea, which was called Fenn Farm. Liz said when we were approaching she felt negativity all around the place but I reassured her that all would be fine.

We set up camp next to two girls and Liz started talking to them, all of a sudden she flipped for no apparent reason and started shouting at me, and throwing things. I don't think the two girls knew what to make of it so quickly disappeared inside their tent and zipped it up. They probably thought *'oh no, we have another domestic going on here.'* I decided to take Liz and Boris for a walk. Liz was extremely agitated and started to shoot things in the sky, she kept telling me that she could see alien ships up above and she was trying to shoot them down. I saw nothing but a clear sky so it was all very strange. All of a sudden, Liz started running away from me in a state of panic, she looked like she had seen a ghost and looked petrified. I tried calling her and by this time had Boris under my arm, as he was still only a puppy. By the time I caught up with Liz she was standing in the middle of the road trying to wave down a car.

I rang the police and explained that I wasn't sure what to do but needed them here urgently as my partner had flipped. I was terrified as wasn't sure how to help Liz. I tried to remain calm and in control as thought if I lose it we have no hope. I saw headlights coming towards Liz and in a split decision chucked the puppy in the ditch and rugby tackled Liz into the ditch too. She had no intention of moving and I was scared for her life. I screamed at her to stay down and not move and prayed that the police would turn up soon. My heart was pounding and the adrenaline went through the roof, I had just saved Liz's life as the car was coming round the bend at a rate of knots and would not have seen Liz in the middle of the road as by this time it was dark.

The police then arrived moments later and handcuffed Liz, she was shouting that it was not her that should be handcuffed, but me. She had totally lost touch with reality and I felt so sorry for her. She looked confused and totally bewildered. The police told me that they were taking Liz to a hospital in Colchester and she would then be assessed.

I went back to the camp site and the two girls were sitting outside their tent, they asked me what had happened so I briefly explained but I didn't want to share too much as that was our own personal business. I packed up the tent and took the puppy home and cried. Again I felt totally helpless.

When I rang the hospital I was told that I couldn't see Liz as she had been heavily sedated and was in no fit state to see anyone. So I had to wait two days before I could go and visit her. This was worse than watching paint dry, because I didn't know what was going on and I was hoping that the doctors were doing the right thing by Liz. It was a scary and worrying time and I felt constantly on edge, which didn't help my anxiety either. I don't know why they feel the need to sedate Liz so much - surely there must be another way.

Liz was discharged after a week although she was still petrified and paranoid that people were after her, that night she had a panic attack so we ended up ringing one of the hospital nurses to reassure her. Once she had the phone call she calmed down a bit but she was still on edge. I kept a close eye on her over the next few weeks and she took some time off work to get better. Her employer was amazing and so supportive especially her boss at the time, Glynis, who looked after Boris when Liz wasn't very well. It was like Boris's second home and he loved it. I took time off work to look after Liz and my work were very supportive and knew about Liz's condition. It was a struggle as financially I don't get paid whilst I am off work but I put money to the back of my mind as the most important thing at the moment was Liz's mental well being. During the time Liz was off work we lost our cat

Billy, to this day we have still not found him. Goodness knows where he went, it was extremely sad and Liz was very upset about this which didn't help her mood. We decided to get another puppy not long after that and named him Charlie Brown, he was supposed to be the quiet one of the bunch! I found that debatable as he was like a hyper child and was constantly on the go. Liz seemed to be recovering well and she went back to work part-time and they had taken a lot of work from her to help her state of mind.

Life got back to an even keel. We went to a friend's wedding in Italy in the summer which was amazing and stayed in the castle grounds, and also visited Rhodes with some friends. I spent a lot of time doing the house up and built a conservatory on the back of the house to give us a bit more room. Having 3 pets in a 2 bedroomed house was quite a snug fit! I needed to be strong for Liz however I was still feeling depressed. I had a lot of past family issues that needed to be addressed and I had still not combated these feelings.

Liz had another mini episode the following year but remained out of hospital and just had a week off work. I advised her to stay away from practicing any spiritual activity as this was making her worse. She agreed and avoided any circles or group conferences. I think the reason that it made Liz worse is that Liz's brain is so very sensitive and she picks up on any spiritual/energy activity. She has a sixth sense and can feel their energies. It is an amazing gift but extremely powerful and if Liz is not well, it heightens excessively and she is taken away to like a different dimension. It's fascinating but also worrying and extremely scary. We weren't particularly looking at moving although the house we were in seemed rather small now. Liz was looking on Right Move one day and went to see a property on the spur of the moment like Liz does. She came back and said that she wanted me to come and view it. It was everything she had asked for and was even on her vision board. Liz is always sending out positive vibes to the universe and constantly says that if you give unconditionally you will get it back tenfold. She does make me laugh when she says this so when this property came up and it was everything she had requested I had to go and view it, just to keep the peace. It was in Coggeshall and Liz was the last person to look at it that day, she fell in love with it straight away. I had my reservations due to the busy road but alas once again she managed to convince me. We put an offer in and this was accepted and sold our other house in Witham within a day. As they say it was meant to be as we moved in to Coggeshall within two months and have now been there for 3 years.

Liz seemed to be much better and we had the family over for Christmas, which was what Liz had always wanted to do since she got the house, with enough room to entertain. We also had a firework party in the November, which was hilarious. All our friends came and Liz's uncle did the food, which was great. We let off the fireworks down at the bottom of our garden, dangerous but fun.

I started to concentrate on the house and decorated the rooms in the colours we wanted. Liz was a little stressed at work as she had been told that her job was being transferred to London and I know she didn't want to go. Unfortunately her boss Glynis had got another job so Liz was being managed by someone else. She missed Glynis and had worked in London when she was younger and didn't want to do it again. We had also moved to the country and commuting was not as easy as what it was before. She made a huge decision and decided to refuse the offer so was therefore made redundant a few months later. One thing I admire about Liz is although she has been through all these episodes she has never been out of a job and has always looked for work without relying on the state for benefits. She found a job pretty quickly after the redundancy and started with an insurance company in Chelmsford. She seemed really happy, if a bit stressed and over worked, however she kept saying she was new and needed to learn loads.

One night whilst we were watching television one of her close friends Nicola rang up in an awful state as she had just had a massive row with her boyfriend who had hit her in an argument. She was distraught and Liz automatically dropped everything and went to her. She packed an overnight bag and said she was going to help her friend. We had a bit of a fall out as I said I didn't want her to go as it would be a risk to her health, but I did understand as it was her friend. I said that I would come and see her the next day. I suppose I didn't realise the full extent of what had happened with Nicola, and when I saw Liz the next day she looked very pale and said that she didn't sleep that well last night. She was adamant that she wanted to stay with Nicola another night just to support her. I agreed even though I was extremely worried about her. The trouble with Liz, is she has this way of convincing you that all is OK and that to stop treating her like a kid. So you have to be a little careful bearing in mind she was 47. The next morning she looked even worse so I stepped in and said to Nicola that she and her son Lewis could stay at ours for the next night as Liz needed to get her sleep otherwise she would relapse. Liz went to work looking like a zombie and I also went to work. The next call I got was from the Human Resources woman at Liz's new company, she was a tad panicky saying that Liz had flipped at work and apparently Liz had told her she had Bipolar and why had no-one told them. I did think to myself that Liz didn't have to divulge anything about her personal medical history but was concerned for Liz so just agreed with the woman. I thought here we go again although I wasn't surprised as Liz was heading that way bearing in mind she had disrupted sleep for the last couple of nights. The HR Woman said that Liz had been taken to A&E for an assessment.

When I arrived and saw Liz in the room on her own, my heart again went out to her, why did this keep happening to her? When she saw me she burst into tears and I gave her a big cuddle. We were left alone for what seemed like ages and chatted about all that had happened.

All of a sudden it seemed like we had the whole medical staff enter the room, there was a social worker, 2 doctors, one nurse, one trainee nurse and me. What a performance I thought. Now I know when this happens why Liz loses patience as she has to repeat the same things over and over again. By now they should have all her notes on the system so why they have to go through all the paperwork and rigmarole again I don't know. Liz becomes extremely frustrated with this. I did think to myself this is going to be interesting.

The social worker started talking to her as if she was a child and I saw Liz's face switch, I find it a bit amusing, because Liz becomes immensely aggressive when people take the piss and also is very intelligent and doesn't suffer fools. She has an amazing insight into her condition and gets frustrated and impatient when people and hospital staff repeat things and treat her like an idiot.

She did eventually calm down so they could all assess her then left us alone again. I always wonder why it takes so long for someone to be assessed; it doesn't help anyone's mental health being shut in a room waiting around. We went to get some water and Liz kicked off again as she could smell smoke on one of the ladies breath on the ward and she didn't think it was appropriate in a hospital. I must admit I did agree with that one. Once back in the room Liz agreed to go to the mental hospital as she knew she couldn't stay in A&E, so we walked calmly down the corridor, all of a sudden Liz flipped again for no reason. All I wanted to do, along with the security guards and social worker was to get her to the mental hospital as she needed help. I didn't want to see my fiancé getting man handled by me or anyone, but I didn't know what else to do. She was screaming and I know now if this happens again I will try and talk to Liz as I didn't realise what was going on in her mind. It must have been terrifying for her and I just didn't think as I thought I was doing the right thing in getting her to the ward.

She was having a massive panic attack so the security guards had to take her back to the room. When I went back in the room she was fuming and was shouting at me, we started rowing and then she ended up punching me in the mouth. I suppose in her head she didn't trust me now although I didn't realise that at the time. I was shocked as wasn't expecting this. The hospital staff opened the door when this happened and I thought *'I can't do this anymore'* so went home. The hospital staff also advised me that they were planning to take Liz to the psychiatric ward as soon as she had calmed down.

I went home in a daze again, fed the animals, attended to my swollen lip, packed Liz's bag and then went back to A&E. I knocked on the door and they advised me that Liz was still there as there was paperwork to be filled out. I went home to bed and returned the next day at 10am. Liz was still in A&E so I started to have a moan and argue as to what and why it was taking so long. I then turned my head and looked across the road and saw Liz being taken in an ambulance by security guards to the mental hospital. She hadn't noticed me and I stood and watched her whilst crying my eyes out. Again I felt helpless and out of my depth.

20

I Will Always Be Here

I returned home feeling crestfallen and empty, the hospital rang me to say that Liz was being assessed and to pop up to the ward later and bring Liz's bag. I waited all morning feeling hollow and hopeless, it was awful to know that Liz was in hospital again and I could have prevented it yet again. I was blaming myself as I suspected the signs once again but didn't react quickly enough, it can happen very fast. I am not sure why either, as Liz is fairly hyper anyhow so it is extremely difficult to sometimes tell the difference. The nurse at the hospital rang a couple of hours later and I took Liz's bag onto the ward. Liz was in solitary confinement as apparently they had no beds on the main ward. This was horrendous as it looked like a padded cell and when I arrived Liz was sitting with her head in her hands on a crash mat in the middle of the room. When the hospital staff opened the door Liz ran towards me and hugged me tightly, she was pleading for me to get her out and saying how horrible it was in a room with 4 walls and no window or fresh air. I did wonder how this room could be helpful to anyone's mental health let alone Liz's. I reassured Liz that she was obviously in here for a reason and the staff, were here to help her. I requested to the staff that Liz have access to a phone in case she wanted to ring me. When I left I didn't want to leave her and I was seriously worried about her state of mind and how she would cope.

Liz rang me a couple of times over the next few hours and I kept reassuring her that everything would be OK. I came back the next day and when I opened the heavy door to where they were keeping Liz I was horrified to what was happening. Liz was banging and screaming on the window that separated her from the hospital staff. She was crying her eyes out screaming *'Let me out.'* I couldn't control myself

I lost my temper and felt my blood rise sky high and shouted at the staff, *'what the fuck are you doing', 'open the door she is not a caged bloody animal!'* When the door opened a distressed Liz ran to me and just slumped into my arms, saying she couldn't cope anymore and she wanted to die. It was awful and extremely upsetting but I had to put my own emotions aside and remain strong and cuddled her tightly and said *'you CAN do this you are a strong person Liz.'* She was sobbing her heart out and said she had no strength left and just wanted to end her life. I couldn't believe it, I started getting upset and we then both ended up crying. I don't think I have ever felt so helpless and totally responsible for what had happened. I should never have left her in the hospital. I felt I was to blame for this, Liz was not suicidal when she went in but this environment had caused her to become so. What is wrong with the system - this was absolutely alarming and a huge worry for future patients.

I carried on reassuring Liz and was now determined beyond belief to get her out of this place. After a lot of negotiating with the hospital staff I managed to get Liz out of the room during the day and back on the main ward so at least she wasn't in isolation. She had to go back and sleep there but at least this helped. I pushed for a meeting with the psychiatrist who was in charge and Liz and I saw him the next day and I explained that being in hospital was making Liz worse and was not good for her mental state. I managed to get the Doctor to agree for Liz to come out during the day and then return at night. We did this for a couple of days and all went well. They then approved for Liz to be discharged back home, which she was over the moon about. She actually skipped out of the hospital as she was so pleased to be free, she said it felt like prison in there and she hated it. I took some time off work to look after Liz over the next few months as unfortunately she lost her job. My employer was very supportive and also offered their support to Liz, which I thought was truly admirable.

Liz seemed to be coping OK considering she didn't have a job, and she started looking for one a couple of months later and luckily her ex-boss Glynis had spoken to Liz's old company and there was an Executive Assistant job available working within another sub division of the company. Liz was thrilled to bits and she got an interview, which cheered her up no end. She was so nervous but apparently the interview went so well that Roy who conducted the interview offered her the job there and then. Liz was due to start in the next 6 weeks and I was so happy and relieved for her as she had been through hell yet again and managed to pick herself up and crack on with life. Liz has got this amazing ability to whatever is thrown at her she takes it on board and deals with accordingly and bounces back each time. I don't know how I would have coped with what she has been through and certainly wouldn't want to either. I have witnessed first-hand how petrified and vulnerable she is and believe me it is heartbreaking to watch.

Liz started the job and seemed to be settling in really well. I was keeping a close eye on her just in case. Later that year we went on a Caribbean cruise, something that we had wanted to do for ages but never got round to it. It was amazing and we had the best time ever. When we got back Liz was a bit high but I just put it down to the holiday. She had a few nights that she struggled to sleep because of the time-zone change but she assured me that she felt fine.

Not long after the holiday, Liz and I were taking the dogs for a walk over the local park, Liz seemed a bit restless and all of a sudden, Liz flipped and started arguing with me, she looked like she had seen a ghost. One of her colleagues from work was in the park and Liz grabbed her and was whispering in her ear. Liz started to throw accusations at me and thought I was about to hurt her. I rang the ambulance straight away which made Liz worse, the work colleague was great and calmed Liz down. Liz agreed that she would only go back in the car with the neighbours, so I rang James and he came and picked Liz up and took her back to his. I drove back on my own feeling isolated and alone again and deeply concerned that Liz had once again gone into an episode. I left Liz with the neighbours for about an hour and when I went round to see her, she seemed to be back to her normal self and was fine with me. It was all very strange, so we carried on as normal for the next hour or so. Liz was gradually becoming agitated later on and was questioning my love for her. I was getting exasperated as I wasn't sure where this was going so I must admit I did flare up which didn't help the situation. Liz flipped again and was worse this time, she was being aggressive towards me and kept going into film mode. What I mean by this is that it seems like Liz acts out parts in films and seems to be like a puppet and doing things so out of character for her. She pretended she was seeing Robbie Williams outside in the garden, and then barking like a dog at something outside the door. I didn't know what was going on, it was like she had lost her mind again.

I tried to avoid ringing the doctors but I felt like things were escalating out of control again and urgently needed help. The doctor arrived pretty quickly after I rang and started to assess Liz, she was becoming increasingly worse and started to do erotic dancing in front of the doctor. In any other situation I would have laughed but this was far from funny and was very scary to watch your loved one doing things that were beyond her control. Liz kept whispering to me that they were all watching her and that we needed to plan our escape. Another two doctors arrived and assessed Liz, the formalities are so regimented and I feel so sorry for Liz as she had to go through the same procedure again and again. No wonder she gets wound up and agitated. Liz then flipped again which sent alarm bells to the doctors and they rang the police and ambulance straight away. Within minutes they arrived, there were 4 of them, 2 police officers and two ambulance staff. I felt helpless again as I watched them take Liz away. I watched from a distance whilst they tried to get her into the police van, she obviously didn't want to go as the next minute I saw the Police officer doing star jumps. I wondered what on earth was happening but thought to myself if anyone can get a police officer to do something then Liz would. I didn't know what context or why it had happened but it worked and they disappeared about 5 minutes later.

I felt totally exhausted and drained of energy. I didn't know how I would cope again with anymore episodes and thought this is it, I can't do this anymore. I loved Liz but this was making me ill too and not good for the health for either of us.

I was told at the time to leave Liz until the next day, so I rang the local hospital and Liz was in the hospital in Chelmsford. I went to visit her along with her good friend Nicola, who was desperate to see her. Liz again looked so sad in the ward and just cuddled us both so tightly. She looked petrified as she was back in the awful place, which she hated. She again pleaded for me to get her out. I knew that she would need to remain there for the next day so tried to calm her down accordingly. Liz recovers remarkably fast from an episode probably because she knows about her condition inside out, having that insight really does help.

Kate, her sister came and visited with me the next day, which I was pleasantly surprised but very grateful for as I knew how much that would mean to Liz. Kate hadn't returned to visit Liz in a hospital setting for the past 10 years or so, this was massive for Liz as well as Kate overcoming her fear of the place too. They hugged and we chatted for ages. Liz was back to herself now, she told us that she had not slept the previous night as she was paranoid that someone was going to get her. I knew how much the hospital affected Liz and made a decision to get her out that day to prevent her mental health deteriorating. She was discharged within a couple of hours, which was brilliant.

I again took some time off work to look after Liz and ensure she ate and slept well. Her company were brilliant and so supportive especially Roy her new boss. He came out to visit Liz along with Gabby the HR lady. I was so pleased as this meant a lot to Liz and helped with her recovery too, as they reassured her that her job was OK.

Liz was back to work within a month and returned on a phased basis. Roy conducted a care plan for her and promised to keep an eye on Liz to ensure she didn't get too stressed.

It's been 10 months now and Liz is doing really well, something happened in March when she went to a meditation that has removed some kind of negative energy. Liz is convinced this was a big part of what she has gone through and I kind of believe it but because I haven't experienced it, personally find it a little hard to believe, but who knows what goes on in our world.

We now have joint therapy to help us deal with Liz's emotions and for me to gain a better understanding on what Liz goes through and I am more patient - which is hard for me! I know that this has made us even stronger and I admire Liz for what she has achieved over the last 10 months. She always turns it around and now does even more talks, blogs, and media coverage to educate and help other people. I am so proud of her and will always support her no matter what is thrown at me.

Liz has also helped me with my emotions and I am pleased to have been able to support her with this book. I think this will really help educate people about the importance of sharing experiences and realise that you are not alone. This book is an extremely brave thing to do for Liz and she has stepped out of her comfort zone in order to make a difference to people's lives.

Both Liz and I live each day to the full and enjoy our time with the dogs and family. I know Liz has Bipolar but it makes her unique and personally I wouldn't change her for the world.

Last Words and How to Contact Me

So there you have it, my open and honest story and people's different perspectives on how it has affected them and what their thoughts are.

I hope you have found this interesting and an eye opener, we feel there are a lot more people out there that suffer in silence and it would be great if they would share their story.

It is really important that people around us are aware and understand the condition. A lot of people who have mental health conditions feel incredibly isolated which can often be worse than the condition itself. It also doesn't help if people are judgemental and think negatively, constantly being told you can't do something can seriously affect someone's mental health. Trying to persuade people to get professional advice with friends and family can be a real help, however they will need to get the proper diagnosis along with the correct medication.

I guess being Bipolar is a bit like living in Tornado Alley in the US, you never know when the next one is going to strike. As long as you have the support from friends and family then all will be OK and with a healthy lifestyle, eating and sleeping properly and staying off drink can hopefully reduce the number and intensity of the episodes.

Kate and I have set up a website in order for people to share stories and we plan to complete talks at events to raise awareness and spread positivity. Also on our website there are links to books/websites which have helped us both in our journey to understand this condition in more detail. We are both learning more and more each day and are so pleased that the Royals have backed mental health with their Heads Together campaign.

Our website is **www.heads2minds.co.uk**, so please feel free to have a browse and let us know any feedback you have or if you are interested in posting your story.

Please sign up to my monthly newsletter to find educational help and also updates on what Kate and I have been up to.

Facebook: **https://www.facebook.com/Heads2minds/**

Email: **lizrotherham@yahoo.co.uk**